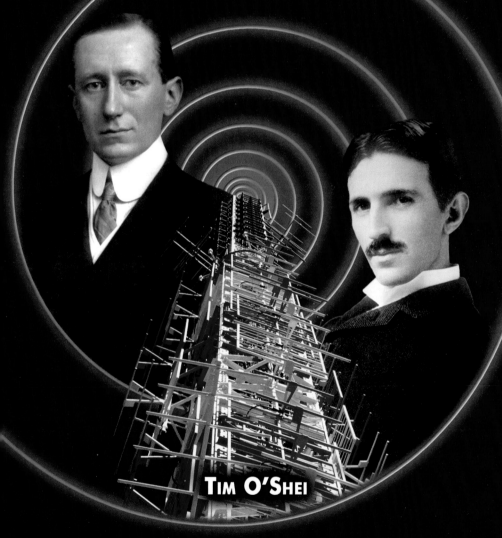

INVENTORS WHO CHANGED THE WORLD

MARCONI AND TESLA
PIONEERS OF
RADIO COMMUNICATION

TIM O'SHEI

MyReportLinks.com Books
an imprint of
Enslow Publishers, Inc.
Box 398, 40 Industrial Road
Berkeley Heights, NJ 07922
USA

To Colin, my future inventor. Keep pushing the limits!

MyReportLinks.com Books, an imprint of Enslow Publishers, Inc. MyReportLinks® is a registered trademark of Enslow Publishers, Inc.

Library of Congress Cataloging-in-Publication Data

O'Shei, Tim.
  Marconi and Tesla : pioneers of radio communication / Tim O'Shei.
      p. cm. — (Inventors who changed the world)
  Includes bibliographical references and index.
  ISBN-13: 978-1-59845-076-7 (hc.)
  ISBN-10: 1-59845-076-X (hc.)
  1. Marconi, Guglielmo, marchese, 1874–1937—Juvenile literature. 2. Tesla, Nikola, 1856–1943—Juvenile literature. 3. Telegraph, Wireless—History—Juvenile literature. 4. Radio—History—Juvenile literature. 5. Inventors—Biography—Juvenile literature. 6. Electric engineers—Biography—Juvenile literature. I. Title.
  TK5739.M3O74 2008
  621.384092'2—dc22
  [B]
                                            2007010043

Printed in the United States of America

10 9 8 7 6 5 4 3 2 1

To Our Readers:
Through the purchase of this book, you and your library gain access to the Report Links that specifically back up this book.
The Publisher will provide access to the Report Links that back up this book and will keep these Report Links up to date on **www.myreportlinks.com** for five years from the book's first publication date.
We have done our best to make sure all Internet addresses in this book were active and appropriate when we went to press. However, the author and the Publisher have no control over, and assume no liability for, the material available on those Internet sites or on other Web sites they may link to.
The usage of the MyReportLinks.com Books Web site is subject to the terms and conditions stated on the Usage Policy Statement on **www.myreportlinks.com**.
A password may be required to access the Report Links that back up this book. The password is found on the bottom of page 4 of this book.
Any comments or suggestions can be sent by e-mail to comments@myreportlinks.com or to the address on the back cover.

♻ Enslow Publishers, Inc., is committed to printing our books on recycled paper. The paper in every book contains 10% to 30% post-consumer waste (PCW). The cover board on the outside of each book contains 100% PCW. Our goal is to do our part to help young people and the environment too!

Photo credits: © Aleksandar-Pal Sakala/ Shutterstock, p. 65; © Charles Taylor, Shutterstock: pp. 78–79; © Joseph Moran, Shutterstock: p. 110–111; © Mary Evans Picture Library/ The Image Works, pp. 14, 60; AmericanHeritage.com, p. 31; AP/Wide World Photos, pp. 5, 53; BBC, pp. 46, 100; CMP Media LLC, p. 102; Columbia University, p. 41; Early Radio History, p. 97; FCC: p. 96; FindLaw.com, p. 103; G4FTC, p. 34; IEEE, p. 115; Library of Congress, pp. 12, 20, 30, 43, 45, 63, 68–69, 70, 80–81, 86–87, 88, 94; MagazineArt.org, p. 61; Marconi Calling, p. 83; Marconi Foundation, p. 32; Mary Evans Picture Library/ Everett Collection, pp. 72–73; Memorial University of Newfoundland, p. 13; Mercurians/ Society for the History of Technology, p. 104; MyReportLinks.com Books, p. 4; National Academy of Engineering, p. 112; National Inventors Hall of Fame Foundation, Inc., p. 37; Nikola Tesla Museum, p. 24; PBS, pp. 10, 89, 108; Photos.com: pp. 8–9, 16–17, 28–29, 48–49, 92–93, 98–99, 106–107; Physicsworld.com, p. 18; Shutterstock: pp. 11, 58, 95; SSPL/ The Image Works, p. 58, 95; Tesla Society: p. 5; Tesla Wardenclyffe Project, p. 66; The Franklin Institute, p. 55; The Marconi Society, p. 109; The Tesla Memorial Society of New York, p. 75; Twenty First Century Books, p. 76; U.S. Early Radio History, p. 82; U.S. Marconi Museum, p. 85; United States Patent Office, p. 59; Wireless World, p. 90.

Cover images: Library of Congress (portraits); Shutterstock.com (tower)

CONTENTS

MyReportLinks.com Books
Great Books, Great Links, Great for Research!

The Internet sites featured in this book can save you hours of research time. These Internet sites—we call them **"Report Links"**—are constantly changing, but we keep them up to date on our Web site.

When you see this "Approved Web Site" logo, you will know that we are directing you to a great Internet site that will help you with your research.

Give it a try! Type http://www.myreportlinks.com into your browser, click on the series title and enter the password, then click on the book title, and scroll down to the Report Links listed for this book.

The Report Links will bring you to great source documents, photographs, and illustrations. MyReportLinks.com Books save you time, feature Report Links that are kept up to date, and make report writing easier than ever! A complete listing of the Report Links can be found on pages 118–119 at the back of the book.

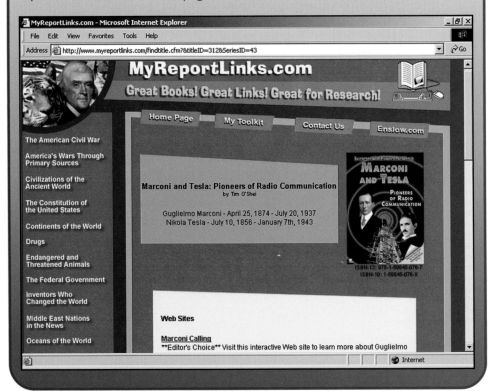

Please see "To Our Readers" on the copyright page for important information about this book, the MyReportLinks.com Web site, and the Report Links that back up this book.

Please enter **MTR1445** if asked for a password.

I do not think there is any thrill that can go through the human heart like that felt by the inventor as he sees some creation of the brain unfolding to success . . . Such emotions make a man forget food, sleep, friends, love, everything.

—Nikola Tesla

Every day sees humanity more victorious in the struggle with space and time.

—Guglielmo Marconi

IMPORTANT DATES

1837 —Samuel F. B. Morse credited with making the first practical telegraph.

1856 —Nikola Tesla is born at midnight between July 9 and 10, in the small village of Smiljan, Croatia.

1863 —Tesla's older brother, Daniel, is killed in a horse-riding accident. Tesla, who is seven years old, begins to see visions that confuse what is real with what is not.

1866 —An 1,800-mile-long cable is laid across the floor of the Atlantic Ocean, connecting the United States with Great Britain. This allowed Americans and Europeans to send messages back and forth using a system called Morse Code.

1874 —*April 25:* Guglielmo Marconi is born in Bologna, Italy.

—*June:* Nikola Tesla graduates from the Higher Real Gymnasium, or the equivalent of high school.

1875 —Tesla begins studies at the Polytechnic Institute in Graz, Austria, in September. There he begins his research on alternating current (AC).

1878 —Nikola Tesla enters the University of Prague, and studies there for one year.

1884 —Tesla moves to the United States and begins working for the Edison Company.

1887 —Marconi enrolls in the Leghorn Technical Institute. This is where his keen interest in the sciences begins to develop.

—German physicist Heinrich Hertz discovers radio waves.

1889 —Tesla signs a contract with Westinghouse Electric Company.

1895 —Marconi sends first wireless signal from a transmitter to a receiver that is set at a distance and cannot be seen. This experiment proved that electromagnetic waves could travel distances.

—Tesla's New York laboratory is destroyed by fire.

1897 —Marconi receives first patent for wireless system. He starts the Wireless Telegraph and Signal Company.

1899 —Marconi successfully sends a message thirty-two miles across the English Channel from Britain to France.

—Tesla sets up a new lab in Colorado Springs, Colorado.

1901 —*January:* The building of a two-hundred-foot-tall transmitter by Marconi's company is completed in Poldhu, England. It is rebuilt after foul weather destroys it in September of the same year. A station is also built in Newfoundland, Canada.

—*December 12:* The first wireless waves are successfully sent from Poldhu, England, to Newfoundland, Canada, using the Morse code for the letter "S."

—Tesla returns to New York and begins construction of his Wardenclyffe laboratory on Long Island.

1905 —Marconi marries Beatrice O'Brien on March 16. They have two daughters and one son together. They divorce seventeen years later.

—Tesla runs out of funding for his Wardenclyffe project and it is abandoned.

1909 —Marconi receives the Nobel Prize for his achievements in radio.

1917 —Tesla is awarded the Edison Medal.

1927 —Marconi remarries.

1937 —*July 20:* Marconi dies at the age of sixty-three due to heart failure.

1943 —*January 7:* Tesla dies at the age of eighty-six.

1983 —Tesla is featured on a United States postal stamp.

—The United States Supreme Court rules that Tesla, along with two other inventors, had priority over Marconi in the invention of radio.

A Transatlantic Plan

Guglielmo Marconi, who loved the spotlight and the attention that it brought, wanted to make a splash. He wanted to accomplish something so big, so astounding, that everyone in the world would want to have a part of it. Marconi was a big thinker. He trusted his instincts, and he was not afraid of taking a risk.

But this idea was a risk—a *big* risk. If it succeeded, it would seize headlines around the world. It would establish Marconi as a worker of wonders and his company as a leader in its field.

If the idea *did not* work, the results could be disastrous. Loads of money would be lost. Untold amounts of trust and confidence would be forever erased.

CHAPTER 1

This was the decision of a lifetime, and Marconi's mind was made up: he was going to do it. Marconi was going to send a wireless signal across the Atlantic Ocean.

→ THE GREAT DIVIDER

Consider the magnitude of such a goal: the blue waters of the Atlantic dominate the western half of the globe. The vast ocean separates what were then (and what many still consider to be today) the two most influential continents on Earth: Europe and North America. For hundreds—even thousands—of years, people had traversed the Atlantic by boat. In 1492, Christopher Columbus sailed the ocean from Europe to the Americas in a search for places to trade spices. The Pilgrims made the crossing in the 1600s, escaping the heavy-handed rule of the king of England. Slaves were packed tightly into boats that churned through the salty waters from Africa and delivered them to plantation owners in North America.

Pirates, warriors, and adventurers have all sailed the Atlantic. Some were caught by storms or icebergs that crushed their boats and sent them to wet, icy deaths. Countless sailors have fallen

American Experience | The Great Transatlantic Cable | PBS - Microsoft Internet Explorer

File   Edit   View   Favorites   Tools   Help

Address   http://www.pbs.org/wgbh/amex/cable/   Go   Links

PBS HOME   PROGRAMS A-Z   SUPPORT PBS   SHOP PBS   SEARCH PBS

THE FILM & MORE
SPECIAL FEATURES
TIMELINE
GALLERY
PEOPLE & EVENTS
TEACHER'S GUIDE

THE GREAT
Transatlantic Cable
AMERICAN
EXPERIENCE

this site....

1870 | JOKES! | Is the cable as   INTERVIEWS | Learn   watch the promo
ientists know in   funny to you as it was   more about the cable,   check local listings

Read all about the laying of **The Great Transatlantic Cable** on this *American Experience* site, a companion to the PBS series. Access a timeline, biographies of the key players, photos of the telegraph, and a selection of related articles.

overboard and become victims of a cold drowning, or perhaps a meal for the sharks that lurk beneath the surface.

Throughout most of American and European history, the Atlantic Ocean was the great divider. Communication between the continents was incredibly slow. Until the mid-1800s, the only way to get a message from North America to Europe was by letter. Since the mail had to be loaded onto a ship, the letter could be weeks old by the time it reached the recipient. Receiving a reply took just as long.

That changed in 1866, when a cable was laid across the ocean floor from Britain to the United States. The transatlantic cable allowed people on both continents to send telegraphs to one another. This was a major development, but it did not quite solve the problem of slow communication. Even when additional cables were laid across the Atlantic's floor, people could not always send messages quickly. There was often a long wait to wire messages on the cables. And that wait time was increased whenever a cable was damaged, which was frequently.

Marconi was determined to tackle the need for quick communication. His idea—his

◀ Before Marconi's advances in wireless communication, people relied on the telegraph to send messages from one continent to another. This photo shows an old-fashioned telegraph machine.

grand goal, the one designed to transform his company, and maybe even change the world—was to send a wireless signal all the way across the Atlantic. Put another way: Marconi was determined to send a message nearly two thousand miles through the air.

The project would be expensive and risky. Marconi's company would have to construct a massive transmitter and receiver in both Europe and North America. And even if those were successfully built, there was no guarantee that they would work. Many scientists believed it was impossible to send wireless messages that far. They thought that the messages would travel straight out of Earth's atmosphere and filter into the nothingness of outer space.

Marconi thought differently. He could

A telegraph operator prints a telegram in this photo taken in 1908.

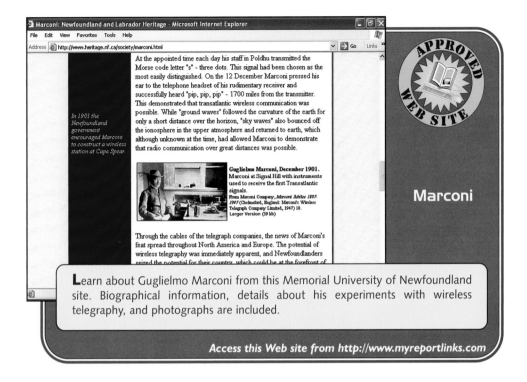

Marconi: Newfoundland and Labrador Heritage - Microsoft Internet Explorer

File Edit View Favorites Tools Help

Address http://www.heritage.nf.ca/society/marconi.html

In 1901 the Newfoundland government encouraged Marconi to construct a wireless station at Cape Spear.

At the appointed time each day his staff in Poldhu transmitted the Morse code letter "s" - three dots. This signal had been chosen as the most easily distinguished. On the 12 December Marconi pressed his ear to the telephone headset of his rudimentary receiver and successfully heard "pip, pip, pip" - 1700 miles from the transmitter. This demonstrated that transatlantic wireless communication was possible. While "ground waves" followed the curvature of the earth for only a short distance over the horizon, "sky waves" also bounced off the ionosphere in the upper atmosphere and returned to earth, which although unknown at the time, had allowed Marconi to demonstrate that radio communication over great distances was possible.

Guglielmo Marconi, December 1901. Marconi at Signal Hill with instruments used to receive the first Transatlantic signals.
From Marconi Company, *Marconi Jubilee 1897-1947* (Chelmsford, England: Marconi's Wireless Telegraph Company Limited, 1947) 18.
Larger Version (39 kb)

Through the cables of the telegraph companies, the news of Marconi's feat spread throughout North America and Europe. The potential of wireless telegraphy was immediately apparent, and Newfoundlanders seized the potential for their country, which could be at the forefront of

Marconi

Learn about Guglielmo Marconi from this Memorial University of Newfoundland site. Biographical information, details about his experiments with wireless telegraphy, and photographs are included.

Access this Web site from http://www.myreportlinks.com

not prove exactly why, but he knew that electro-magnetic waves emitted on Earth stayed on Earth. In previous experiments, he had sent messages at long enough distances to confirm for himself that the waves stayed within the planet's atmosphere.

⊙ SECRET PROJECT

Work began quietly. Marconi insisted that everyone involved keep the project a secret. He chose Poldhu, England, as the site for erecting his two-hundred-foot-tall transmitter. Once that was completed in January 1901, he took a ship to the United States. There he decided to build his other station in Cape Cod, Massachusetts. Progress was fairly smooth until September 1901, when gale winds ripped apart the Poldhu station. Then in November, the Cape Cod antenna suffered a similar fate.

His project in ruins, Marconi decided to try again. His crew rebuilt the Poldhu station. But instead of constructing a new station at Cape Cod, Marconi moved the project to Newfoundland, Canada. This time, he did not attempt to build a station that matched the one in England. Instead, he and his team would simply raise an antenna into the air using kites and balloons.

On Tuesday, December 10, Marconi and his assistants cabled a telegraph to Poldhu. They were ready to begin. The plan was simple: each afternoon, Poldhu would repeatedly send the Morse code for the letter "S." If Marconi's team heard the "dot dot dot" in Newfoundland, then the transatlantic signal had been successfully received.

For the first two days, Marconi's team heard nothing. The weather was giving them trouble by pulling the kites up and down. With the antenna

▽ *Marconi and his associates are shown raising the receiving antenna by kite at St. John's, Newfoundland, in December 1901.*

constantly changing altitude, it was little surprise they heard nothing.

The big event happened at half past noon on December 12. Marconi was listening and heard a trio of quick clicks. Shocked but encouraged, Marconi asked his assistant, George Kemp, to listen. He, too, heard the "dot dot dot." For the next couple of hours, the signal kept coming through. Success! Marconi's wireless waves had conquered the Atlantic!

Meanwhile, a New York City-based inventor named Nikola Tesla kept tabs on Marconi's demonstration. Tesla knew that Marconi's success was also his own, because Marconi's equipment was developed using radio components invented by Tesla.

One of Tesla's engineers said to him, "Looks as if Marconi got the jump on you." Tesla responded, "Marconi is a good fellow. Let him continue. He is using seventeen of my patents."[1]

Perhaps Tesla thought he would get credit in due time. But it would not be so simple.

SMART YOUNG SCIENTISTS

CHAPTER 2

Guglielmo Marconi was born in the Italian city of Bologna on April 25, 1874. His father, Giuseppe, owned an estate called Villa Griffone, which was nestled on a hill near the Apennine Mountains. Guglielmo's mother, Annie, came from a family of Irish whiskey makers. She was seventeen years younger than her fifty-one-year-old husband and much more energetic and adventurous. While Giuseppe preferred to stick close to Villa Griffone, which had once belonged to his father, Annie enjoyed traveling. Whenever she could—and especially when the weather turned cold—Annie packed up and visited relatives in other parts of Europe. Guglielmo and his brother Alfonso, who was nine years older, were her companions.

SMART, BUT NOT A "STUDENT"

Annie and her sons spent a lot of time in England, where they had relatives. They also traveled to other parts of Italy. One of their favorite destinations was a port town called Leghorn. Italian navy sailors bantered about town, and their ships dotted the water. The sailors, their ships, and the sea intrigued Guglielmo. He developed a deep passion for ocean travel, one that would stick with him for life.

All of this traveling made it difficult for the Marconi boys to attend a traditional school. Instead, the Marconis hired their own teacher for Guglielmo and Alfonso. Teaching Guglielmo was surely a frustrating task: he was quite smart, but easily bored. Guglielmo was not a sit-and-study kid. He preferred building a contraption, dreaming up a scientific experiment, or playing near the sea. Guglielmo loved the water. He even had a small sailboat—a gift from his father—that he used to sail around the port of Leghorn.

While Guglielmo did not like desk work, he loved to read. Giuseppe Marconi had a large library of books at Villa Griffone. Whenever he could,

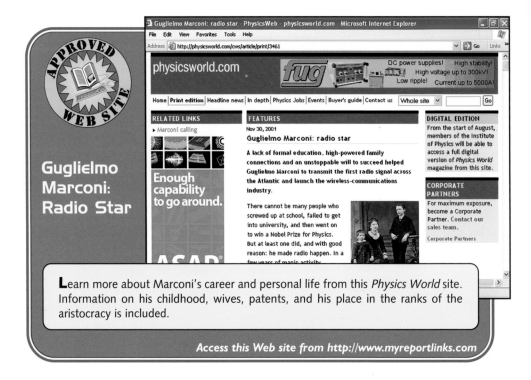

APPROVED WEB SITE

Guglielmo Marconi: Radio Star

Learn more about Marconi's career and personal life from this *Physics World* site. Information on his childhood, wives, patents, and his place in the ranks of the aristocracy is included.

Access this Web site from http://www.myreportlinks.com

Guglielmo slipped among the stacks of books and set his imagination free as he read stories of Greek gods and heroes. He also enjoyed reading about his hero, the American inventor Benjamin Franklin.

Like most future inventors, Guglielmo's mind was packed with ideas. He liked to tinker with toys and tools to build something new. One time, he wired a metal rod on the roof of a home to a bell inside. He wanted to see if he could capture energy from lightning to ring the bell. During the next thunderstorm, that is precisely what happened.

Another time, Guglielmo made his cousin Daisy cry by turning her sewing machine into a contraption designed to cook meat. Guglielmo was particularly close to Daisy and didn't want to upset her, so he undid his work. Soon, Daisy had her sewing machine back. She also had gotten a glimpse of her cousin's ability to take an existing piece of technology and transform it into something new *and* useful. This is the ability that would one day make Guglielmo famous. But at times it also made his father furious.

⊖ STRICT EXPECTATIONS

Giuseppe Marconi was strict. He expected Guglielmo and Alfonso (and an older son, Luigi, from a previous marriage) to work and study hard. Guglielmo was certainly a hard worker, but he preferred to apply himself to his own projects. He didn't even attend traditional school until age twelve. When he finally did attend school like other children, he became bored. Moving from class to class and sitting at a desk while listening to a teacher lecture didn't capture his interest. Guglielmo was also very shy, which made it difficult for him to find and keep friends. Other children teased him because he spoke Italian but had a British accent, which made him different from them. He enjoying fishing, playing the piano, and toying with inventions—all things a person does by himself.[1]

Guglielmo's goal was to enter the Naval Academy, located in Leghorn. Students were considered for

This map of Europe from 1898 shows Marconi's birthplace of Bologna, Italy, as well as Leghorn, where he studied at the Leghorn Technical Institute. It also shows the location of Gospić, Croatia, where Tesla lived as a child. In the 1860s, Croatia was part of the Austro-Hungarian Empire.

admission to the academy around the time they became teenagers. Guglielmo did not get in—his grades were not good enough. He was heartbroken, and so was his father. Giuseppe felt that Guglielmo had been spending far too much time inventing and experimenting. He felt that all these activities had taken Guglielmo away from his schoolwork, and he was angry at both his son and his wife for it.

With the Naval Academy no longer an option, in 1887 Guglielmo enrolled in a school called the Leghorn Technical Institute. He was not particularly excited about the place until he started taking science classes. Those classes captured his interest so deeply that his mother hired a teacher to give him extra science instruction.

Guglielmo wanted to study science in college, but he failed to gain admittance to the University of Bologna. His impatience for school—and his resulting poor grades—were still holding him back. His father's disappointment continued. But then luck struck the Marconis. A prominent professor named Augusto Righi lived nearby. Annie convinced the professor to allow Guglielmo to work with him. The match was perfect: Righi's specialty was Guglielmo's top interest—electricity.

⇒ BORN IN THE STORM

Nikola Tesla was born at midnight between July 9 and 10, 1856, in the tiny village of Smiljan, Croatia, then part of the Austro-Hungarian Empire. He was born during a storm. Fittingly, thunder and lightning crackled in the sky as Nikola came into the world.

➡A Creative Young Inventor

Nikola's father, Milutin, was a priest in the Serbian Orthodox Church. The Reverend Tesla was highly educated and knew several languages. He wrote and could recite poetry from memory. He taught Nikola how to strengthen his memory by teaching him to recite poems after hearing them only a single time. He also taught Nikola how to perform mental math rather than using paper.

Nikola's mother, Djuka (DOO-kuh), had little education but was perhaps the smartest member of the family. She had an impressive memory. Like her husband, Djuka loved to memorize and recite poetry. She took care of Nikola and his four siblings, which left her little personal time. But in the spare moments she had, Djuka was a creative inventor. She often took household items and improved or combined them to create a handy device that made chores go faster.

Like his mother, Nikola was an enthusiastic inventor. One time, he connected a wooden disk to a pair of sticks. He glued four June bugs to the disk and as they tried to fly, he watched them make it spin. Another time, Nikola and his older brother Daniel created a small water turbine in a pond. He also invented a frog-catching hook. He took a piece of a wire and used stones to pound it into a hook. At first, Nikola found that he could not get any frogs to lunge out of the water and bite his hook. He made a quick adjustment and instead offered the hook to frogs that were already out of the water. They bit! This was an early sign of Nikola's creative problem-solving abilities.

Though he may not have realized it at the time—he was only five—the frog hook was an important lesson for young Nikola: an invention is only good if you make it useful. A good invention allows you to do something new or to do an old job more easily. Throughout his life, Nikola would struggle with this. His most important inventions are still in widespread use today. But some of his grandest ideas are not, mainly because people could not figure out a way to make them useful.

→ Peace in the Quiet

Some of Nikola's most creative and productive moments came while he was sitting alone. Quiet surroundings cleared Nikola's mind. This allowed him to focus on his creative ideas and develop inventions inside his head. But a state of peaceful-ness was not easy for Nikola to reach.

In 1863, Nikola's older brother Daniel was killed while riding the family horse. Nikola was seven at the time. Daniel's death set off visions in Nikola's

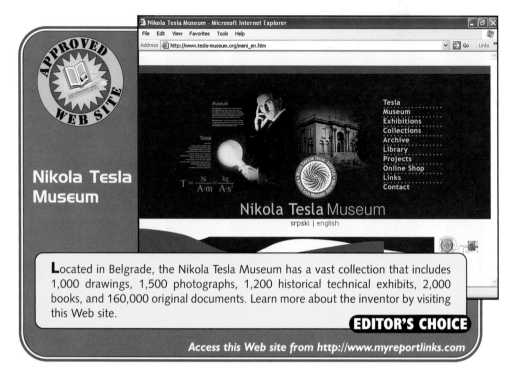

APPROVED WEB SITE

Nikola Tesla Museum

Located in Belgrade, the Nikola Tesla Museum has a vast collection that includes 1,000 drawings, 1,500 photographs, 1,200 historical technical exhibits, 2,000 books, and 160,000 original documents. Learn more about the inventor by visiting this Web site.

EDITOR'S CHOICE

Access this Web site from http://www.myreportlinks.com

mind. He saw scenes from the past, but sometimes they looked so real that he became confused. Was he imagining the past or seeing something for real? Often, he couldn't tell. Nikola's older sister Milka helped him work through these visions. She could do little more than talk to him, but that helped her brother to calm his mind.

Reverend Tesla wanted to move the family to a new home in a new town. He hoped the move would give the family a fresh start and help them get away from the haunting memories of Daniel's death. The family moved to the town of Gospić. Nikola was lonely there—he had no friends, and he missed living near the woods and water. But then, one day not long after the family moved to Gospić, Nikola became a small hero.

During a firefighting demonstration for the whole town, the firefighters were having trouble getting their hose to work. Nikola had a feeling that the hose, which was fed into the river, was kinked. He jumped in the water, swam down to the hose, and discovered he was right. It was indeed kinked. Nikola straightened the hose and swam up to the surface. The townspeople cheered. Young Nikola Tesla had saved the day!

IMPROVING HIMSELF

Nikola's first school in Gospić was the Normal School, which is the equivalent of an elementary school. His middle school was called Gymnasium. At Gymnasium, Nikola had the chance to use a variety of equipment in science class. Now some of the concepts he had envisioned in his head or built in rough form at home were sitting on a desk in front of him. He used the opportunity to learn more science and to improve his approach to life.

Nikola read a novel called *The Son of Aba* and decided that he needed to develop stronger self-control and discipline, like the main character in the book. He started to work on this by not allowing himself to have things he wanted. For example, his mother packed his favorite fruit into his lunch. Instead of eating it, Nikola gave it away and watched his friend munch on the fruit. Exercises like this taught him patience and self-control, which paid off.

One of Nikola's final acts before graduating was dealing with a teacher whom he thought was unfair. Nikola thought his math grade was too low. To prove it, he asked the director of the school to make up an incredibly difficult math test. The director did, and Nikola nearly aced it. The director changed Nikola's grade. People were impressed by the grown-up manner in which fourteen-year-old Nikola dealt with the unfair grade. Respect for him grew. Nikola was asked to work in the town library, a job he loved because it gave him easy access to many books.

⮕ SCIENTIST ... OR MINISTER?

Nikola was planning to enter high school, called the Higher Real Gymnasium. Not all students attended high school back then, and Nikola's father did not want him to go. He wanted him to become a minister—a job that didn't require an education at the Higher Real Gymnasium.

The idea made Nikola physically sick. He did not want to become a minister. He wanted to pursue science. He wanted a chance to take the ideas in his head and turn them into real inventions. Reverend Tesla finally gave in when he received a letter from his cousin, who lived in Karlovac. Karlovac was where the Higher Real Gymnasium was located. The cousin suggested that Nikola could stay with her when he moved there for school. Reverend Tesla decided that it was a sign he should let Nikola go. Nikola quickly started feeling healthier. He was going to school after all!

Nikola enjoyed learning at the Higher Real Gymnasium, but he missed home. He enrolled in extra classes and finished the four-year curriculum in three years. He also decided to pursue the field of electricity. He graduated in June 1874 with plans to become a scientist. Reverend Tesla was not happy with that decision—he wanted Nikola to become a minister. But that idea still depressed Nikola. He became ill, and it seemed almost as if he didn't want to live anymore. Nikola had become infected with cholera, a deadly disease that was spread mainly by contaminated water. Reverend Tesla realized that his son was also deathly depressed.

"Perhaps," Nikola suggested, "I may get well if you will let me study engineering."

Reverend Tesla thought about it and agreed. If letting Nikola pursue his dream would save his life, then so be it.

"You will go to the best technical institution in the world," Reverend Tesla replied.[2]

Nikola was thrilled! Thanks in part to his good spirits, he quickly recovered. Science was in his future.

Wireless Works!

As Marconi worked with Professor Righi, he spent much of his spare time devouring books in the University of Bologna library. He read about the 1,800-mile-long cable that had been laid across the floor of the Atlantic Ocean in 1886. The cable connected the United States with Great Britain, allowing Americans and Europeans to send messages back and forth in a matter of minutes. To use this telegraph, operators relied on a system called Morse code. Every letter of the alphabet was represented by a series of long and short clicks.

Chapter

3

Today, with telephones and computers instantly connecting almost every part of the globe, this Morse code telegraph system would be viewed as dreadfully slow. But back in the late 1800s, it saved many days' worth of time. Before the transatlantic cable, the only way to communicate between Europe and the United States was to send a letter by ship.

Not surprisingly, however, the cable was often in need of repair. Marconi wondered whether it might be

possible to send messages across the ocean without any
wires at all.

The thought, at that time, seemed nothing more than
magical. But it was actually a very scientific question, and
a challenge worth pursuing. Guglielmo Marconi would
soon find that out.

➔ WAVES IN THE AIR

During a summer 1894 vacation with his mother in the
Alps, Guglielmo came across a science magazine article

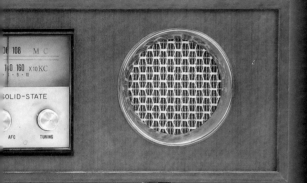

written by his friend Professor Righi. The article
described the work of a
scientist named Heinrich
Hertz, who had recently
died. Seven years earlier
Hertz had conducted
experiments that proved
electrical waves can move through the air.

Hertz's work was based on earlier experiments conducted by another scientist, James Clerk Maxwell.
Maxwell and another scientist, Michael Farraday, had
shown that electricity and magetism were related.
When put together, they caused vibrations.

Hertz took their work one step further by building an
apparatus that demonstrated how electromagnetic
waves could travel from one place to another. Marconi
wanted to transmit those waves over longer distances

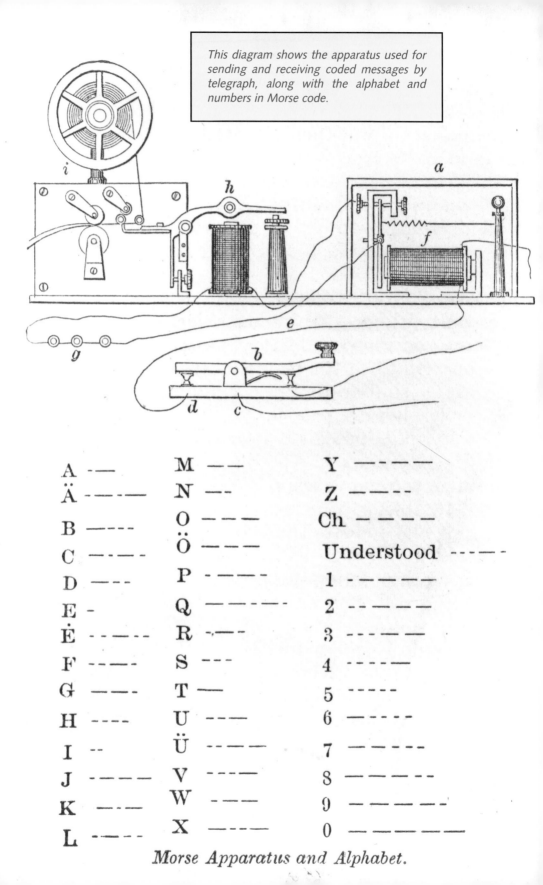

This diagram shows the apparatus used for sending and receiving coded messages by telegraph, along with the alphabet and numbers in Morse code.

A	·—	M	——	Y	—·——
Ä	·—·—	N	—·	Z	——··
B	—···	O	———	Ch	————
C	—·—·	Ö	———·	Understood	···—·
D	—··	P	·——·	1	·————
E	·	Q	——·—	2	··———
Ė	··—··	R	·—·	3	···——
F	··—·	S	···	4	····—
G	——·	T	—	5	·····
H	····	U	··—	6	—····
I	··	Ü	··——	7	——···
J	·———	V	···—	8	———··
K	—·—	W	·——	9	————·
L	·—··	X	—··—	0	—————

Morse Apparatus and Alphabet.

Marconi thought the idea was so simple that he was surprised nobody had already achieved it. "It seemed difficult to believe no one else had thought of putting it into practice," Marconi said.[1]

When Marconi told Righi about his ideas, the professor scoffed. It was a waste of time, Righi said. Scientists already know that electromagnetic waves can travel. But trying to send them over long distances would be fruitless.

Marconi disagreed with this thinking. The concept was clear in his mind: electromagnetic waves could help people communicate from far away. He was determined to pursue the idea, with or without help from anyone.

American Heritage: The Cable Under the Sea

Written twenty years ago, this *Invention & Technology* magazine article provides some insight into the problems associated with laying the transatlantic cable across the North Atlantic.

Access this Web site from http://www.myreportlinks.com

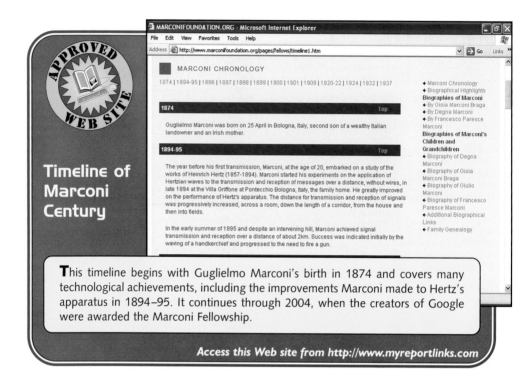

Timeline of Marconi Century

MARCONIFOUNDATION.ORG - Microsoft Internet Explorer

File   Edit   View   Favorites   Tools   Help

Address http://www.marconifoundation.org/pages/fellows/timeline1.htm

MARCONI CHRONOLOGY

1874 | 1894-95 | 1896 | 1897 | 1898 | 1899 | 1900 | 1901 | 1909 | 1920-22 | 1924 | 1932 | 1937

1874   Top

Guglielmo Marconi was born on 25 April in Bologna, Italy, second son of a wealthy Italian landowner and an Irish mother.

1894-95   Top

The year before his first transmission, Marconi, at the age of 20, embarked on a study of the works of Heinrich Hertz (1857-1894). Marconi started his experiments on the application of Hertzian waves to the transmission and reception of messages over a distance, without wires, in late 1894 at the Villa Griffone at Pontecchio Bologna, Italy, the family home. He greatly improved on the performance of Hertz's apparatus. The distance for transmission and reception of signals was progressively increased, across a room, down the length of a corridor, from the house and then into fields.

In the early summer of 1895 and despite an intervening hill, Marconi achieved signal transmission and reception over a distance of about 2km. Success was indicated initially by the waving of a handkerchief and progressed to the need to fire a gun.

- Marconi Chronology
- Biographical Highlights
Biographies of Marconi
- By Gioia Marconi Braga
- By Degna Marconi
- By Francesco Paresce Marconi
Biographies of Marconi's Children and Grandchildren
- Biography of Degna Marconi
- Biography of Gioia Marconi Braga
- Biography of Giulio Marconi
- Biography of Francesco Paresce Marconi
- Additional Biographical Links
- Family Genealogy

This timeline begins with Guglielmo Marconi's birth in 1874 and covers many technological achievements, including the improvements Marconi made to Hertz's apparatus in 1894–95. It continues through 2004, when the creators of Google were awarded the Marconi Fellowship.

Access this Web site from http://www.myreportlinks.com

Annie Marconi had always been her son's biggest supporter. She knew that if he was going to experiment with electromagnetism, he would need his own laboratory. Fortunately, the Villa Griffone was a large home. Annie helped her son set up a laboratory in the attic. Marconi's father, Giuseppe, was not happy about this, but Annie believed in her son and wanted him to pursue his ideas. With her help, Giuseppe relented. He allowed the attic to become a lab, and Professor Righi loaned Marconi some equipment.

Once his lab was set up, Marconi got to work. His first step was re-creating Hertz's experiment. He connected a battery to an iron bar wrapped in wire, creating an electromagnet, which was, in turn, connected to a transmitter. This contraption was set up a few feet from a second arrangement that included a battery, a bell, and a tube of iron filings called a coherer.

To travel far, electromagnetic waves need to be long and strong. This is one of the reasons that Professor Righi, among others, first believed that Marconi's work with long-distance wireless would be fruitless. The professor did not see how such waves could be produced. But the earth's atmosphere is actually full of electricity—only scientists did not yet know this.

⊜ LESSONS FROM A THUNDERSTORM

One day Marconi was experimenting in his attic laboratory while a thunderstorm raged outside. He noticed that the iron filings inside his coherer started sticking together. The bell to which they were attached began to ring. The thunderstorm was sending electromagnetic waves through the air, and the lightning was miles away. This proved that the waves could travel great distances.

With the lesson learned during the thunderstorm serving as encouragement, Marconi kept improving his equipment. Eventually his attempt at emulating Hertz's experiment was successful: the battery and electromagnetic waves emitted a spark of energy that traveled from the transmitter to the second contraption. When the electrical charge hit the tube, the iron filings stuck together and conducted the electricity to the bell, which rang.

Marconi knew this was only the beginning. So far he had simply re-created what Hertz and other scientists had already done; he had not accomplished anything new. His goal was to figure out a way to transmit these electromagnetic waves over long distances.

Always thoughtful and organized, Marconi was persistent in trying to improve his apparatus. He tried different sizes of glass coherer tubes, and he

See an actual reconstruction of the attic laboratory at Villa Griffone as it looked in the spring of 1895 when Marconi successfully sent his first wireless signal from his parent's home. Learn more about Marconi and explore the house and grounds of **Villa Griffone: The Birthplace of Wireless** through the photographs on this site.

experimented with using different types of metal filings inside the tubes. He varied the types and sizes of metal plates connected to the spark transmitter. Little by little, he made progress. The signals were traveling farther and farther—across the attic, to different floors of the house, and finally from inside to outside.

IMPRESSIVE PROGRESS

At first, his family was not impressed. Marconi spent all hours in his laboratory, rarely coming downstairs to eat and taking only an occasional break to sleep. Annie had taken to leaving trays of food outside the attic door. So at first, when Marconi was only making a bell ring from one side of the attic to the other, his progress did not seem like that big a deal—at least not considering all the time he was spending holed away in his makeshift lab.

But as Marconi began sending the signal farther and farther, from one floor to another, and finally from indoors to outdoors, it became obvious that he was doing something significant. He even added an antenna for distance and a small hammer so that the transmitter could send Morse code signals.

His mother was impressed. His cousin Daisy, whom Marconi showed how his wireless worked while she was visiting, was amazed. Giuseppe was also beginning to realize that his son had quite a future in science.

It was in 1895 that Marconi realized his wireless work was a true success. One day, he had his brother Alfonso and a couple of farmers carry the receiver far away from the laboratory. Marconi stood in the window watching until he could no longer see them. By then they were about a mile away. They worked out an arrangement that once the receiver was out of sight, Marconi would tap on the transmitter. If the signal reached the receiver, Alfonso would aim the rifle he was carrying toward the sky and fire a shot. That shot would signal success.

Marconi tapped the transmitter. Moments later, he heard a shot. It worked! As he suspected, electromagnetic waves *could* travel distances. This was significant news—it proved that the waves could be received even when the receiver was out of sight of the transmitter. Though Marconi did not realize it at the time, this is because the earth's ionosphere, a layer of the earth's atmosphere, is electrically charged. When radio waves travel through the atmosphere, they are reflected toward the earth by the ionosphere.

⊜ Seeking Support

Once Marconi transmitted a wireless signal over the distance of a mile and around objects, it was clear that he had an invention worth developing. But he could no longer do it alone. Marconi would need a top-level laboratory and a budget to pay for equipment and helpers.

Annie, of course, remained eager to help her now twenty-one-year-old son. Giuseppe was also excited about wireless technology and threw his support behind his son. The family wrote to the Italian postal service to see if the telegraph officials there were interested in helping to develop wireless technology. A disappointing letter came back: the Italians saw no use or need for wireless.

Annie next suggested trying to find supporters in London, England. Her family still lived there, and they were both well-known and wealthy. Annie wrote to her family and told them that she and Guglielmo would be coming. They arrived via

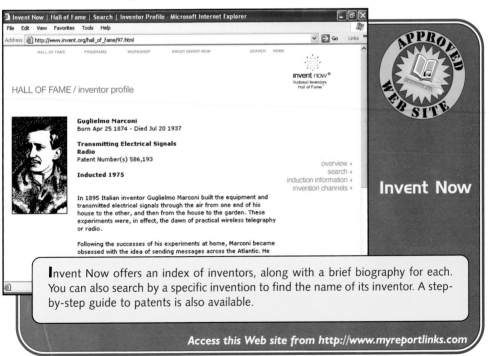

Invent Now offers an index of inventors, along with a brief biography for each. You can also search by a specific invention to find the name of its inventor. A step-by-step guide to patents is also available.

Access this Web site from http://www.myreportlinks.com

train in early 1896. Annie's thirty-three-year-old nephew, Henry Jameson-Davis, received them at the train station.

An engineer, Jameson-Davis was particularly interested in his cousin's invention. Marconi had his wireless equipment packed in two black boxes— one contained a transmitter, the other a receiver. But before Marconi put on a demonstration for his cousin, he had to fix his equipment. Unfortunately, a curious customs guard had roughly poked through the pair of boxes, wondering what the unusual tubes and wires were designed to do.

⮕A Life-Changing Meeting

On the other hand, when Jameson-Davis saw what those boxes *could* do, he was impressed. He took his cousin to see a lawyer, who told Marconi to apply for a patent. The lawyer knew right away that wireless communication would be a valuable tool, and Marconi needed to protect himself and make sure no one could steal his ideas. The patent process was long and involved, and required lots of detailed paperwork and drawings.

Jameson-Davis also introduced Marconi to a man named A. A. Campbell-Swinton. An expert in electricity, Campbell-Swinton liked Marconi and his ideas. He introduced Marconi to the chief engineer of the British post office, William Preece. For Marconi, this was to become a life-changing meeting.

Preece, sixty, was one of England's earliest telegraph engineers. He truly understood the importance of wireless communication, particularly for ships. People on land could use telegraphs or, by the late 1800s, telephones. Sailors had neither of those options to rely on in case of trouble. If a storm struck a ship at sea, causing it to sink or throw people overboard, there was no way to call for assistance. The captain simply had to hope another vessel would pass by, see the situation, then stop and help.

About a dozen years earlier, Preece had unsuccessfully tried to develop wireless technology. Marconi mentioned Preece's attempts in a letter to his father. "[Preece] seemed to show extreme interest in my case," Marconi wrote, "and told me how he had tried to do what I have achieved using an arrangement different from mine without obtaining any good results."[2]

➡A Natural Showman

Preece's wireless system required parallel wires to run on each side of the water—something that would not be practical for long distances. Preece was very interested to see how Marconi's system worked. When Marconi successfully demonstrated it for him, Preece smiled. The chief engineer promised the young inventor that he would help him in every way possible.

Beyond registering for a patent—which Marconi received in 1897—one of the best ways for an inventor to lay claim to a new technology is to demonstrate it publicly. A successful public showing creates a buzz. Stories appear in newspapers, word spreads by mouth, and people start associating the inventor's name with the invention.

Marconi was a natural speaker who felt comfortable in the spotlight. Throughout his life he would put on plenty of shows. Preece helped him arrange one of the first. In July 1896, with English post-office officials watching, Marconi set up his transmitter on a rooftop. One mile away, his receiver sat atop another building. The transmitter clicked, the receiver responded. Postal officials were wowed. Despite the distance and several buildings obstructing the way, the signal was clear.

During the next several months, Marconi put on similar demonstrations for military officials and newspaper reporters, among others. Marconi quickly became the best-known name in the field of wireless communications. Newspapers called him the "inventor of wireless."[3]

An Italian Welcome

After an 1897 demonstration in which he sent a signal nearly nine miles across water, Marconi was invited back to Italy. By now, the Italians realized that they never should have passed up the opportunity to work with him nearly two years earlier. Marconi demonstrated his "black boxes," as they were known, for government and military officials and even for the king and queen. From a naval base, he sent a message to a ship that was eleven miles away at sea.

In 1897, Marconi started the Wireless Telegraph and Signal Company. His cousin, Henry Jameson-Davis, was the managing director. Marconi owned 60 percent of the business, while investors paid money to own the rest.

Preece was unhappy to see Marconi form his own company. He had hoped they could continue working together. Now, the British post office formed its own wireless service to compete with Marconi.

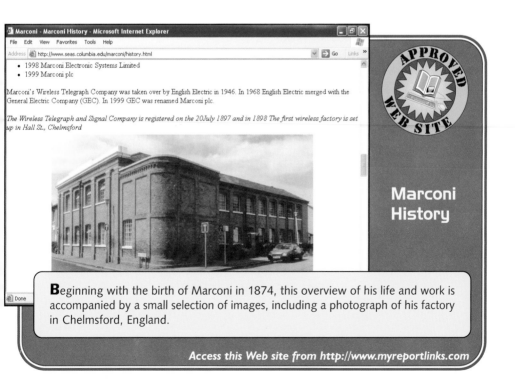

Marconi - Marconi History - Microsoft Internet Explorer

File   Edit   View   Favorites   Tools   Help

Address   http://www.seas.columbia.edu/marconi/history.html   Go   Links »

- 1998 Marconi Electronic Systems Limited
- 1999 Marconi plc

Marconi's Wireless Telegraph Company was taken over by English Electric in 1946. In 1968 English Electric merged with the General Electric Company (GEC). In 1999 GEC was renamed Marconi plc.

The Wireless Telegraph and Signal Company is registered on the 20July 1897 and in 1898 The first wireless factory is set up in Hall St., Chelmsford

Marconi History

Beginning with the birth of Marconi in 1874, this overview of his life and work is accompanied by a small selection of images, including a photograph of his factory in Chelmsford, England.

Access this Web site from http://www.myreportlinks.com

Many inventors did not tend to make good businessmen. Their best talents were taking concepts that most people could never grasp—like using electricity to send sound through the air—and turning them into real devices. Generally speaking, these inventors didn't always make sound business decisions.

A Savvy Business Decision

Marconi was different. He was a smart, savvy entrepreneur who had clear goals. He decided to focus specifically on creating ship-to-ship wireless technology. While he knew he could create more of his "black boxes" for land communication, most places were wired with telephone and telegraph lines. Marconi knew that competition would cut into his profits. Ships, on the other hand, could not be wired. Wireless communication was their only option, and Marconi was best positioned to provide it.

The decision was a good one, but much work remained. Marconi and his staff moved to the English shore in November 1897. In a popular vacation spot called the Isle of Wight, Marconi set up an office in a hotel.

Before they could sell wireless technology to the militaries and shipping companies, he and his staff had to make sure it worked quickly and easily. They also had to make sure that wireless messages could travel far distances, since ships in distress are often many miles away from other ships. The Marconi crew had to figure out how to make wireless work well in both good weather and under stormy conditions, so they often worked in the rain. Marconi's staff built a one-hundred-and-twenty-foot antenna outside and got to work.

A couple of months after setting up on the Isle of Wight, Marconi built another testing station inland. This one was located in Bournemouth, where in 1898 a group of newspaper reporters were covering a story about England's prime minister. When a blizzard crushed the area with snow and damaged telegraph wires, the reporters had no way of transmitting stories to their newspapers. No way, that is, until Marconi offered his wireless service.

As the reporters wrote stories about Marconi's wireless system, interest grew. During a ship-wreck near one of Marconi's testing sites, wireless equipment was used to call for a lifeboat. The value of wireless communication was becoming clear, both for lifesaving and news making. An Irish newspaper asked Marconi to provide minute-by-minute reporting on a popular boat race. Marconi

This photo from 1916 shows a ▷ U.S. Army Signal corpsman receiving a wireless message on a wagon.

rode on a boat that trailed the racers. Throughout the race he sent hundreds of updates to his assistant, George Kemp, on shore. Kemp then phoned the updates to the newspaper.

Marconi's fame was growing. England's Queen Victoria had Marconi set up a wireless system for her to use during a vacation. The queen loved the contraption and sent several dozen messages.

American newspapers were beginning to take notice, especially when, in March 1899, Marconi successfully sent a message thirty-two miles across the English Channel from Britain to France. Later that year, Marconi took his first trip to the United States. He had been invited to cover another boat race, and the people were so excited that a young woman led a huge crowd of fans by yelling, "Three cheers for Marconi!"[4]

Marconi also demonstrated his wireless boxes for the U.S. military. Though the tests did not run perfectly, they did give Marconi a chance to show the lifesaving potential of wireless. During one of the tests at sea, a person fell overboard. The wireless was used to immediately call a smaller boat to rescue the victim. Without the wireless, the person would certainly have drowned.

A Transatlantic Splash

As famous as Marconi was becoming, his company was not yet making money. In fact, near the turn

Taken in approximately 1903, this photo shows Marconi seated at a desk.

of the century, the Marconi company was nearly bankrupt. Developing wireless technology was expensive and tedious. One problem was always followed by another challenge.

For example, a key issue that Marconi had to resolve was interference. Often, one wireless signal crisscrossed with another. When that happened, the two signals played over each other. The result was a jumbled message that made no sense. Marconi had to figure out a way to broadcast a signal that was tuned to a single frequency. By 1900, he had figured out how to do it. Still a

This site celebrates the centennial of Marconi's groundbreaking first transatlantic signal that traveled from Cornwall, England, to St. John's, Newfoundland, on December 12, 1901. Access photographs, articles, timelines, interviews and more on **BBC: Marconi 100.**

EDITOR'S CHOICE

bigger challenge tickled Marconi's mind. He wanted to send a signal across the Atlantic Ocean.

Marconi insisted that everyone involved keep the transatlantic project secret—even if they had to lie. A British journalist asked Marconi about the mysterious project: "Is there any truth in reports that you are contemplating the sending of messages between this country and America?"

"Not in the least," Marconi replied. "I have never suggested such an idea, and though the feat may be accomplished someday, it has hardly been thought of here."[5]

In truth, of course, the goal was dominating Marconi's mind. Even he was a little surprised when that Morse code "S" finally crackled through on December 12, 1901. Marconi turned to his assistant, Kemp, and handed him the earpiece. "Do you hear anything, Mr. Kemp?" he asked.[6]

Kemp, too, heard the "dot dot dot." For the next couple of hours, the signal kept coming through. Success! Marconi's wireless waves had conquered the Atlantic. Now that his experiment had worked, Marconi decided to tell the world about it. Newspapers everywhere published stories about the wireless message. Scientists around the world congratulated Marconi. Telephone inventor Alexander Graham Bell hosted a celebration dinner for him in New York City. This was big news indeed!

POWERFUL VISIONS

In April 1875, Tesla prepared to go to Graz, Austria, to attend the Polytechnic Institute. At around the same time, Nikola received a government notice requiring him to join the army. (All eighteen-year-olds were required to serve.) Nikola's father was concerned that his son was not healthy enough to handle military life. And he had already lost one son. So Reverend Tesla was determined to keep Nikola out of the military. He sent Nikola to hide for several months in a cabin in the mountains. During that time, Reverend Tesla used family connections to get Nikola released from military service.

That September, Tesla was cleared and allowed to go to the Polytechnic Institute. He worked hard and long, waking each day at 3:00 A.M. to begin studying. Unlike other students, Tesla socialized little. He avoided dating. Tesla feared that relationships would distract him

CHAPTER 4

from his studies. He viewed his time at the Polytechnic Institute as a way to prepare for a lifetime of invention and creation. He was determined to get the most out of it.

Tesla's professors noticed his hard work and became worried about it. One of them actually wrote to Reverend Tesla to say that the professors were concerned Nikola was working too hard. Nikola did not know about the correspondence between his father and the professor until several years later. He discovered the letters while sorting through some papers after his father had died.

In Professor Poeschl's class, Tesla learned about a motor designed by Thomas Edison to generate direct current. Tesla told the professor he thought it would be possible to build an alternating-current motor. Direct current could not travel far before losing power. But Tesla believed alternating current could travel a great distance because the electricity traveled as a wave, instead of in a straight line.

The professor dismissed the idea. Others, he said, had tried to build such a motor. They all failed. Alternating current, he said, was a dead idea. "Mr. Tesla may accomplish great things,"

Professor Poeschl told the class, "but he certainly never will do this."[1]

Nikola did not believe it, and he was determined to prove himself right.

Alternating Current (AC)

In September 1878, Tesla entered the University of Prague. He studied there for a year, but his father died the next summer. That left the Tesla family with only a little money. Nikola could not afford to stay in school. He had to get a job. Tesla found one in Budapest, Hungary, with the Central Telegraph Company. His first position involved simple, dull duties. Tesla worked hard, however, and soon he was given the bigger responsibility of designing telephone equipment.

During this time, Tesla also spent considerable energy testing alternating-current motors. He was not actually building them, but rather designing and testing them inside his mind. Tesla's unusual ability to visualize was so strong that he could see and remember even the tiniest of details about an invention in his head. He could test and adjust a contraption—all in his mind.

Overworked and Exhausted

Tesla's job and his AC project had him working long days. He slept only two or three hours a night. He did not eat well, and almost never exercised.

Soon Tesla became sick. As he had as a child, he began seeing strong visions in his head. He grew very sensitive to sounds and movement. "For a while," Tesla later wrote: "I have [given] myself up entirely to the intense enjoyment of picturing machines and devising new forms. It was a mental state of happiness about as complete as I have ever known in life."[2]

His friend Anital Szigety told Tesla to get outside and exercise more. They started going for daily walks. The exercise and companionship was the perfect remedy: Tesla quickly started to feel better. His body was rested, and his mind was clearer. During one of their walks on a particularly warm and pleasant day, Tesla stopped abruptly. Szigety wondered what was wrong. Tesla stood still and silent for several moments, then announced that he had finally come up with a way to harness alternating current. Tesla used a stick to draw a diagram in the dirt. He explained that an armature, or rotating part, could be used to create a circling magnetic force that would produce more electricity than direct current.

⊜ Joining Edison

At age twenty-six, Tesla moved to Paris to work for the Continental Edison Company, the European arm of the American inventor's company. His job was to travel around Europe, fixing various problems at power plants. During a trip to Alsace, France, Tesla spent all his spare time building the AC motor he had planned in his mind. It worked, and Tesla was anxious to start showing off his invention and working to build the public's excitement.

⊕A Promise Not Kept

But first he had to finish the job in Alsace, where a railroad station lighting plant had gone bad. He worked hard to get the lighting station back in order, then returned to Paris. Tesla's bosses had promised him a handsome bonus for fixing the Alsace plant, but when he asked for it, he got no results. One executive sent him to another person, who sent him to a third, who claimed to be unable to help and sent him back to the first.

Tesla felt betrayed. He had been counting on that money to buy materials and equipment to continue building and testing AC motors. Now, he found himself without the funds for this work. Tesla quit the job.

One of the company officials, Charles Batchelor, was troubled to see Tesla go. He knew the inventor had remarkable intelligence and talent. He suggested that Tesla head to New York City and try to get a job working for Thomas Edison himself. Batchelor, who knew Edison, even wrote the famous inventor a note on Tesla's behalf.

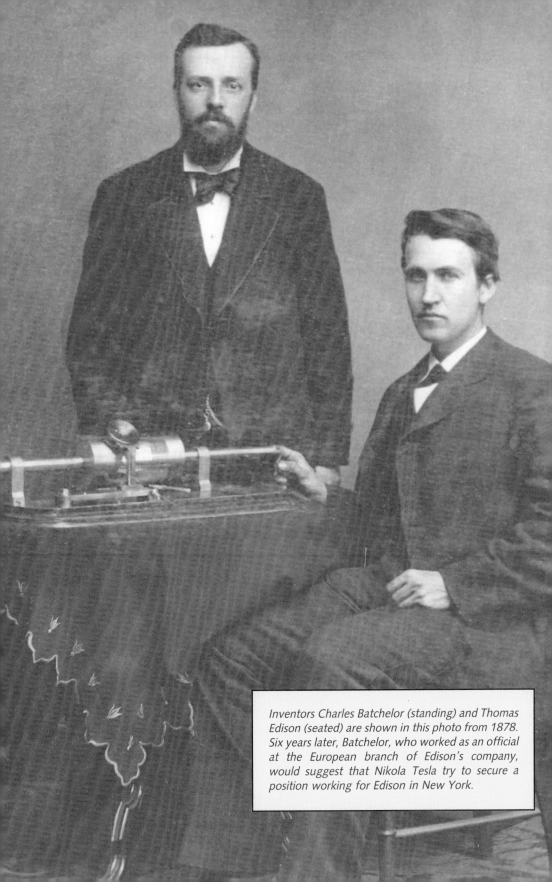

Inventors Charles Batchelor (standing) and Thomas Edison (seated) are shown in this photo from 1878. Six years later, Batchelor, who worked as an official at the European branch of Edison's company, would suggest that Nikola Tesla try to secure a position working for Edison in New York.

⊜ TESLA'S ARRIVAL IN NEW YORK

In 1884, Tesla took a ship across the Atlantic to New York City. He arrived with only four cents. A pickpocket had taken his wallet or it had been lost—he was not sure which—while he had been taking a train to the dock in Europe.

As Tesla made his way through the busy streets of New York, which were jammed with pedestrians and crisscrossed with electrical wires above, he noticed a store owner throwing a fit. Tesla asked what was wrong. The businessman explained that he could not get one of his machines to work. Tesla said he could probably fix it—and in less than an hour, he did. The happy store owner gave Tesla twenty dollars and offered him a job. Tesla took the money but declined the offer—he wanted to work for Edison.

⊜ EDISON'S CHALLENGE

When Tesla arrived at Edison's office, he walked into a bustling scene of commotion. Edison's company had lighting systems installed all over New York—on streets, in businesses, and in private homes. But there were many problems. Sometimes the lighting systems burned out for seemingly mysterious reasons. At other times, wires caught fire. Edison's engineers were frequently sent out to fix these problems. They were kept very busy attending to repairs.

When Tesla entered Edison's office, all of the engineers were out. Two more emergency calls had just come in. One was for the Vanderbilt mansion, an expensive New York home where the lighting wires had caught fire. The other was from the *Oregon,* an ocean liner that was docked in New York and about to depart for Europe. The lights on the *Oregon* had suddenly gone out.

A very stressed Edison was heading to the Vanderbilt mansion to tend to the overheated wires. Upon meeting Tesla, he took a few moments to

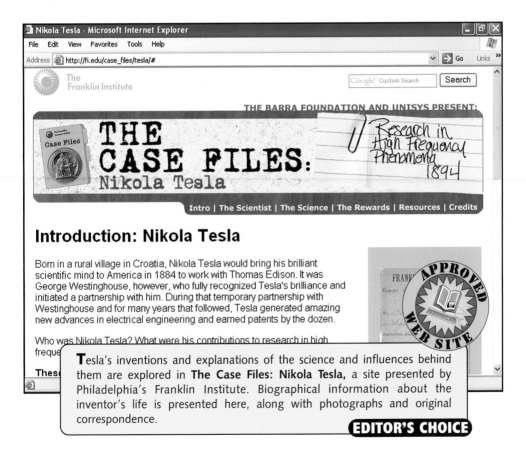

Nikola Tesla - Microsoft Internet Explorer

File   Edit   View   Favorites   Tools   Help

Address   http://fi.edu/case_files/tesla/#   Go   Links »

The Franklin Institute

Google™ Custom Search   Search

THE BARRA FOUNDATION AND UNISYS PRESENT:

THE CASE FILES: Nikola Tesla

Case Files

Research in High Frequency Phenomena 1894

Intro | The Scientist | The Science | The Rewards | Resources | Credits

Introduction: Nikola Tesla

Born in a rural village in Croatia, Nikola Tesla would bring his brilliant scientific mind to America in 1884 to work with Thomas Edison. It was George Westinghouse, however, who fully recognized Tesla's brilliance and initiated a partnership with him. During that temporary partnership with Westinghouse and for many years that followed, Tesla generated amazing new advances in electrical engineering and earned patents by the dozen.

Who was Nikola Tesla? What were his contributions to research in high freque

Thes

APPROVED WEB SITE

Tesla's inventions and explanations of the science and influences behind them are explored in **The Case Files: Nikola Tesla,** a site presented by Philadelphia's Franklin Institute. Biographical information about the inventor's life is presented here, along with photographs and original correspondence.

EDITOR'S CHOICE

read Batchelor's note. "My Dear Edison," Batchelor had written. "I know two great men and you are one of them. The other is this young man."[3]

Edison was interested, but wanted to see for himself that Tesla was as good as Batchelor said. He sent Tesla to the *Oregon* with orders to fix the lighting so the ship could head to Europe. Tesla went to the ship and worked straight through the night. By dawn, the *Oregon* was relit and ready for travel. Tesla reported back to Edison's office with the news. And with that, he had a job.

Tesla spent incredibly long days working for Edison. He typically began around 10:30 A.M. and worked straight through to 5:00 A.M. the next morning, pausing only to eat dinner. Edison, who also worked long hours and slept little, appreciated Tesla's efforts. But he did not agree with Tesla's focus on alternating current. Edison preferred his direct-current system. This would one day lead to a showdown between the two genius inventors.

⊛ BAD BREAKS AND FRUSTRATIONS

Tesla's professional life was full of bad breaks and bad luck. He told Edison that he could make the company's dynamos work better. Edison offered Tesla fifty thousand dollars to do it. Several months later, Tesla completed the project and asked Edison for his money. Edison refused, telling Tesla the offer had only been a joke.

"You are still a Parisian," Edison said. "When you become a full-fledged American, you will appreciate an American joke."[4]

Tesla quit angrily. Now twenty-nine, he needed a new job. He still wanted money to develop his alternating-current motors, and he was hoping to find businessmen who could provide him with the resources to make it happen. He was excited when a group of businessmen approached him to form the Tesla Electric Light Company. Tesla's first job was to improve arc lighting, which he did. With that task completed, Tesla expected to be given the funds to conduct his alternating-current research. But the businessmen provided little money, and Tesla was soon out of the company.

A Genius Digging Ditches

After this long line of setbacks, Tesla simply needed a job to earn money to live on. In 1886, he found one digging ditches. The job paid two dollars a day. Nikola was frustrated. He knew that his ideas were good, but he couldn't find anyone with the money and belief to help him. So there he was, stuck digging ditches.

Finally, his luck changed. Tesla's boss from the ditch-digging crew helped him meet a man named A. K. Brown, who managed the Western Union Telegraph Company. Brown was shocked that a genius was digging ditches. Brown formed a new company, named it after Tesla, and told the scientist to get to work developing alternating current. The Tesla Electric Company opened a laboratory on Fifth Avenue in New York City.

By 1888, Tesla had secured more than thirty patents for his electrical equipment. He spoke about the possibilities of electricity in a speech to the American Institute of Electrical Engineers. Newspaper reporters wrote about Tesla, and the public began to become aware of his work. People started debating whether Edison's direct current or Tesla's alternating current would be better. Of course, few

This photo, taken in 1887 ▶ or 1888, shows Tesla's working model of his AC induction motor. The motor uses two alternating currents to create a rotating magnetic field that makes the rotor turn.

A diagram from Tesla's 1888 patent application for a dynamo electric machine.

(No Model.)   2 Sheets—Sheet 1.

N. TESLA.

DYNAMO ELECTRIC MACHINE.

No. 390,414.   Patented Oct. 2, 1888.

Fig.1

WITNESSES: INVENTOR
Raphael Netter   Nikola Tesla
Frank G. Hartley   BY
                                                         Duncan, Curtis & Page
                                                                 ATTORNEYS

people understood the difference.

Edison promoted direct current and criticized alternating current every chance he got. His supporters jumped on any opportunity to make alternating current seem bad or dangerous. When alternating current was used to put a man to death in prison, Edison's supporters began to call it the "executioner's current." Edison was much more famous than Tesla, so many people believed him.

⊜ Westinghouse's Deal With Tesla

However, a smart businessman named George Westinghouse believed in Tesla. Westinghouse, whose company manufactured a variety of equipment, visited Tesla in 1889. He was impressed with Tesla's work and made an offer: he wanted to buy Tesla's patents for alternating-current motors. The payment would be $1 million, plus a royalty for every AC motor that Westinghouse sold. Within days, a check and a contract arrived, and Tesla signed it. He spent much of the next year working in Pittsburgh, Pennsylvania, teaching Westinghouse engineers about his equipment.

The deal made Tesla rich and gave him the chance to pursue his research as he had always

Author Mark Twain is shown holding a loop over a resonating coil in 1895. High-tension current passes through his body before creating the light. Tesla is shown in the background on the left.

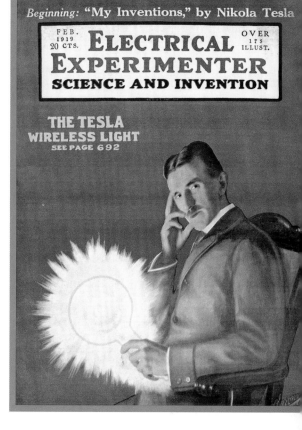

The February 1919 issue of Electrical Experimenter featured Tesla's wireless light and an installment of My Inventions, his autobiography.

dreamed. The 1890s were the most productive decade of Tesla's career. He developed wireless electric lamps and technology that improved motors and X-rays. His most important invention during that time was the Tesla coil, a transformer that safely changed low voltage to high voltage. Most types of electronic equipment, such as radios and televisions, have a Tesla coil.

Nikola was often invited to give presentations and interviews, and to attend parties. After many months of busily traveling and talking, he grew sick. He spent several weeks recovering and decided to stop spending so much time on sharing his work with others. Tesla realized he would rather be in his laboratory, creating, testing, and fine-tuning new inventions.

→WESTINGHOUSE NEARS BANKRUPTCY

Tesla had many quirks. He disliked earrings, pearls, and touching the hair of others. He found overweight people to be gross. When he walked, he counted his steps. When he sat down to eat, he calculated how much food was on his plate. Tesla liked to do things in groups of three. He was intensely private and did not like visitors interrupting his lab work.

One day in 1892, George Westinghouse dropped by the laboratory. With stress etched across his face, Westinghouse told Tesla that he was close to declaring bankruptcy. The Westinghouse company had run out of money. Much of the reason, Westinghouse said, was the royalties that the company was paying to Tesla. Westinghouse was hoping Tesla would agree to change the deal. "Your decision determines the fate of the Westinghouse company," the businessman said.[5]

Tesla had always been grateful to Westinghouse for supporting his work. Tesla had also long been interested in seeing alternating-current power spread around the world, but he was not as interested in money. He viewed this as a chance to help a man who had once helped him. Tesla told

George Westinghouse is shown in this portrait dated between 1900 and 1914.

Westinghouse that he wouldn't hold him to the contract.

"You have always been my friend," Tesla said. As a show of faith, Tesla took the contract in his hands and ripped it apart. Westinghouse gave Tesla a $216,000 settlement. Many historians, however, question whether Tesla ever received the payment.

A Mistake Worth Millions

Tesla did not realize at the time what a tremendous mistake he had made. By destroying his Westinghouse deal, Tesla threw away millions of dollars in future royalty payments. If he had truly wanted to give up something in order to help Westinghouse, there were other ways he could have done it. For example, he could have renegotiated the contract and received a lower royalty. Or he could have changed the agreement to allow Westinghouse to withhold royalty payments for a period of time until the company was financially strong. But Tesla was not business smart. He was a brilliant inventor, but when it came to deal making, he had little ability.

⊜ GRAND VISIONS, LIMITED FUNDS

Giving back his future royalties meant Tesla would have limited money for the rest of his life. This affected his ability to invent: never again could Tesla afford all the equipment he wanted.

Still, Tesla never lost his grand visions. In February 1893, Tesla began making presentations to groups of scientists about the possibilities of wireless communication. He said that the earth's atmosphere—specifically the ionosphere—was electrically charged. It could be used to transmit sound messages. Tesla demonstrated his idea to a group of scientists in St. Louis, who watched him send a message from a transmitter to a receiver thirty feet away.

Meanwhile, the battle between Tesla's alternating current and Edison's direct current continued. Tesla was largely considered the winner in 1893, when Westinghouse's alternating-current system was chosen over Edison's equipment to light up the

At the 1893 World's Columbian Exposition, Tesla demonstrated his device called "the Egg of Columbus." This device proved the principles of the rotating magnetic field and the induction motor. The copper egg spun on its major axis and stood on end due to gyroscopic action.

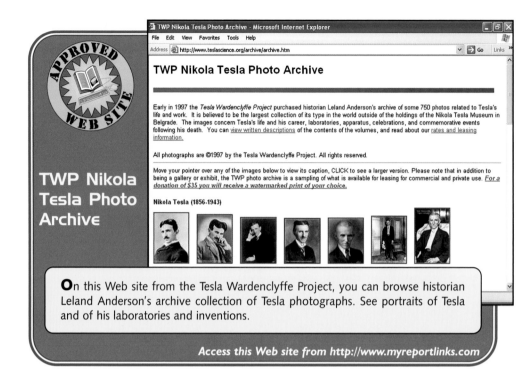

TWP Nikola Tesla Photo Archive

On this Web site from the Tesla Wardenclyffe Project, you can browse historian Leland Anderson's archive collection of Tesla photographs. See portraits of Tesla and of his laboratories and inventions.

Access this Web site from http://www.myreportlinks.com

World's Fair in Chicago. Crowds were mesmerized by the spectacle of a city shining in the night under the lights. Newspapers around the world ran photographs. This showcased for the world just how safely and effectively alternating current worked.

Tesla put on a show at the fair. He used electromagnetic energy to make a metal egg spin. He used wireless energy to light up bulbs he held in his hand.

⊜POWERING NIAGARA

In the mid-1890s, Tesla helped Westinghouse set up an electric plant at Niagara Falls, New York.

Massive turbines captured the power of the water. Transformers sent that power to generators that lit up Niagara Falls and, soon after, the city of Buffalo, twenty-two miles away. Buffalo became known as the "City of Light." In 1903, Tesla's generators lit Buffalo for the Pan-American Exposition. But years before that, Tesla's alternating current was solidly ahead of Edison's direct current.[6]

In the mid-1890s, Tesla continued developing experiments that wowed—and sometimes scared—people. In his New York City laboratory he began working with vibrations. He used a machine called an oscillator, which caused vibrations of varying strengths. One day, he turned his oscillator so high that he broke walls and windows as far as two blocks away. This happened in the middle of the night, and people thought there was an earthquake. (It would have been very unusual, as earthquakes rarely hit New York City.) The police arrived at Tesla's lab, quite unhappily, but the experiment was over.

Quietly, Tesla was thrilled with the power of his experiment. But it had caused enough trouble to convince him not to do it again in New York City.

⊝A Lab In Ruins

At half past two in the morning on March 13, 1895, a policeman knocked at the door of Tesla's home. There was a fire in his lab. Tesla followed the police to his lab, which was completely ruined. All his equipment, all his experiments, all his notes—everything was gone. Tesla did not have the funds to rebuild the lab by himself, but a few months later, a businessman named Edward Dean Adams spent $100,000 to help Tesla build a new lab on Houston Street.

Still, the fire was a major setback. Among the notes Tesla lost were those that dealt with wireless transmission. Tesla had been planning to publicly

demonstrate the capabilities of his long-distance wireless system, but now he could not.

Meanwhile, Marconi started demonstrating his own wireless technology in 1895. It appeared to many people that Marconi was using Tesla's ideas, but Marconi insisted that his work was original. Tesla seemed unconcerned at the time. His ideas were still recorded in his mind—surely he could rebuild what the fire had destroyed.

Tesla's work in wireless was slowed, but not stopped. He built a remote-controlled boat that could follow commands sent through the air. In 1898, Tesla demonstrated how his boat worked for a large crowd inside New York's Madison Square Garden. He also developed an idea for controlling weapons such as missiles by remote control. Nowadays, these are known as guided missiles.

Tesla's generators lit up Buffalo for the 1903 Pan-American Exposition.

Nikola Tesla at approximately age thirty-eight.

➔ LAB IN THE MOUNTAINS

In 1899, an attorney who worked for George Westinghouse offered to help Tesla set up a lab in Colorado Springs. In this lightly populated town nestled in the mountains, Tesla could perform much larger electrical experiments than he could in tightly packed New York City. Tesla accepted the offer, moved to Colorado, and oversaw the construction of a large lab. The most prominent features were a massive Tesla coil, a seventy-foot outdoor tower, and a two-hundred-foot pole with a copper ball on top. These would be used in Tesla's efforts to harness electricity and transmit wireless messages. This equipment could handle 12 million volts of electricity and create sparks that jumped 135 feet.[7]

➔ TESLA'S EXPERIMENT CAUSES AN UPSET

Tesla took full advantage of his time in Colorado Springs, working long hours and spending large amounts of the money provided to him. Most of his heavy-duty experiments were performed at night so that he did not strain the Colorado Springs' power system.

Sometimes, however, even that plan didn't work. One night, inspired by a recent lightning storm, Tesla and his assistant cranked up the power flow into the Tesla coil, which channeled the electricity into the two-hundred-foot pole.

This publicity photo from 1900 shows Tesla seated in his Colorado Springs lab while several million volts of lightning are discharged by a large Tesla coil. The photo is called a double exposure because one image, that of Tesla in the lab, is superimposed over the other, the voltage discharge. (Tesla was not actually in the lab when the lightning was discharged.)

High above the pole, bolts of man-made lightning decorated the sky. It worked! Tesla had created lightning. As Tesla admired his work, however, all of it collapsed into black. The lightning stopped, and the night air was silent.

Tesla soon learned that he had blown out the Colorado Springs generator. The townspeople were upset. Tesla fixed the generator with his own time and money, but this was one of his final experiments in Colorado Springs.

The businessmen who funded Tesla's research were growing unhappy with his ideas. Tesla had suggested to them that he might be able to capture the earth's natural electricity and use his equipment to make it free to anyone, anywhere. Doing this, he figured, would save people from paying high electrical bills. But the businessmen were not keen on this idea. If people did not pay electrical bills, then the electric companies would go out of business. And that would cost businessmen—people like them—enormous amounts of money. They were not ready to support plans like that, so Tesla was about to run out of money.

⬡ COMMUNICATIONS CITY

By 1901, Tesla was back in New York City. He still had big ideas but virtually no money to pursue them. Tesla's grandest idea was to build a massive communication center that was capable of sending messages to anywhere in the world. Tesla wanted to build an entire city around this center. In other words, he wanted to build a "communications city."

"One of the immediate consequences," he said, "will be the transmission of messages without wires, over sea or land, to an immense distance."[8]

Such a project demanded massive amounts of land and money. But the list of people to whom he could turn for money was getting shorter. Many wealthy businessmen had already invested in Tesla

Above: Transmitting Tesla Tower and Laboratory built in 1901-1905 by Stanford White, famous architect and Tesla's friend. Located in Wardenclyffe, Long Island. This was to be the first broadcasting

See the transmitting tower and lab built in Wardenclyffe, Long Island, by Tesla's friend, architect Stanford White. The **Tesla Memorial Society of New York** site includes many other photographs and information about obtaining books and tapes about Tesla's life.

and had been unhappy with the return. However, J. P. Morgan was willing to listen.

Morgan was one of the richest men in America. He invited Tesla to his home and listened to the inventor's ideas for a communications city. Morgan was not convinced it would work, which meant he was not going to invest any money. Tesla presented Morgan with another idea for funding: would Morgan be interested in buying 51 percent of the rights to Tesla's patents? Morgan *was* interested in this—he would be purchasing something, not just risking money on an idea.

Morgan paid Tesla $150,000, and Tesla set to work. He decided to call the city Wardenclyffe.

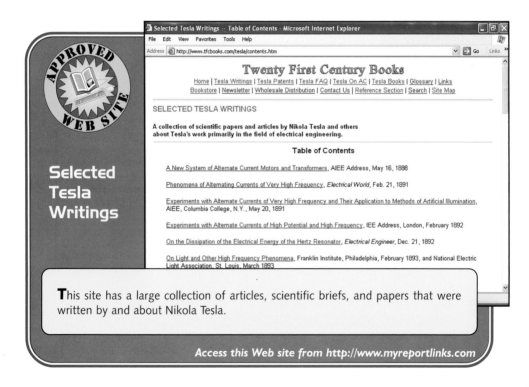

Selected Tesla Writings

Selected Tesla Writings -- Table of Contents - Microsoft Internet Explorer

File   Edit   View   Favorites   Tools   Help

Address http://www.tfcbooks.com/tesla/contents.htm

Twenty First Century Books

Home | Tesla Writings | Tesla Patents | Tesla FAQ | Tesla On AC | Tesla Books | Glossary | Links
Bookstore | Newsletter | Wholesale Distribution | Contact Us | Reference Section | Search | Site Map

SELECTED TESLA WRITINGS

A collection of scientific papers and articles by Nikola Tesla and others about Tesla's work primarily in the field of electrical engineering.

Table of Contents

A New System of Alternate Current Motors and Transformers, AIEE Address, May 16, 1888

Phenomena of Alternating Currents of Very High Frequency, *Electrical World*, Feb. 21, 1891

Experiments with Alternate Currents of Very High Frequency and Their Application to Methods of Artificial Illumination, AIEE, Columbia College, N.Y., May 20, 1891

Experiments with Alternate Currents of High Potential and High Frequency, IEE Address, London, February 1892

On the Dissipation of the Electrical Energy of the Hertz Resonator, *Electrical Engineer*, Dec. 21, 1892

On Light and Other High Frequency Phenomena, Franklin Institute, Philadelphia, February 1893, and National Electric Light Association, St. Louis, March 1893

This site has a large collection of articles, scientific briefs, and papers that were written by and about Nikola Tesla.

Access this Web site from http://www.myreportlinks.com

He bought two thousand acres of land on Long Island and began construction of a large brick laboratory building and a one-hundred-and-eighty-seven-foot tower with a huge dome on top. He soon needed more money, and Morgan loaned it. But funding could not take care of another problem—supplies. Tesla's project required large numbers of motors, dynamos, and other equipment that was not readily available in those days. This slowed his progress.

Tesla tried to get people excited about his project by advertising his vision. He wrote about being able to send news, music, pictures, or messages anywhere in the world. Nowadays, those things *are* constantly available through technology like television, computers, and cell phones. But back then, none of those things existed, and people simply did not grasp the possibility. They heard what Tesla was saying, but they couldn't foresee his vision becoming reality. In many ways, Tesla was far ahead—maybe even one hundred years ahead—of his time.

By 1902, Morgan stopped loaning money. The Wardenclyffe project crumbled and was abandoned in 1905. Tesla's dream died.

WIRELESS BECOMES WIDESPREAD

CHAPTER

5

A·M

Marconi worked hard and fast during the years following his 1901 transatlantic signal. He needed to improve wireless technology so that it could be easily and affordably installed on a ship or boat. He needed it to be reliable so that a captain knew if his vessel got in trouble, the wireless equipment would work. One of the most notable improvements Marconi made was replacing the glass coherer tube—which easily broke when rough waters rocked a ship—with a magnetic rod.

Few people knew how to operate Marconi's wireless equipment effectively. Until there was a steady supply of operators, Marconi knew his equipment would never get widespread use. Marconi addressed this need by opening a school called the Radiotelegraphy Institute. The school trained people to operate Marconi's equipment.

Marconi's company built wireless stations in Novia Scotia, Canada, and Cape Cod, Massachusetts.

The company also improved the station at Poldhu, England. These three high-powered stations would make it much easier to transmit wireless signals.

By late 1902, Marconi was able to send full messages between England and Canada. During the next few years, his company started selling radio service to ship operators and governments. The Marconi company provided its own equipment and operators who worked aboard the ship.

Ships began using wireless technology to find out news that was happening around the world during a voyage. That news was published in a newspaper that was distributed to passengers. Those passengers could also send a wireless message from the ship to the shore. The message was then sent to the recipient by a traditional telegraph. So if a ship was ahead of schedule, for example, passengers could send a message to their families at their destination and tell them to expect an early arrival. Other companies offered services similar to Marconi's. He was so competitive that he would not allow his operators to handle messages sent to and from other companies.

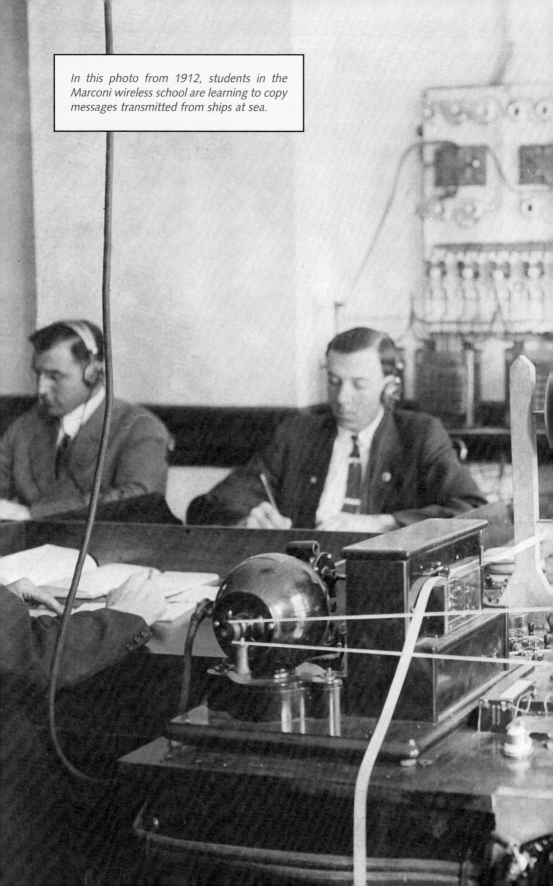

In this photo from 1912, students in the Marconi wireless school are learning to copy messages transmitted from ships at sea.

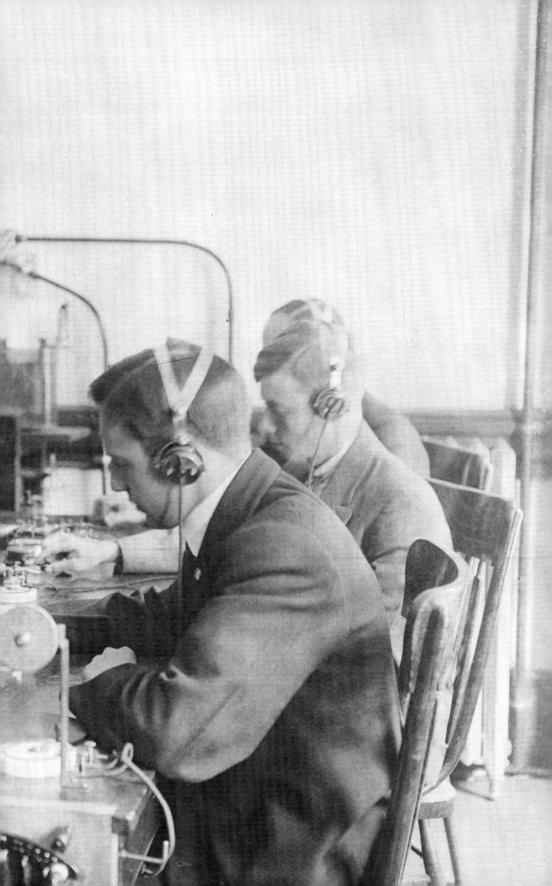

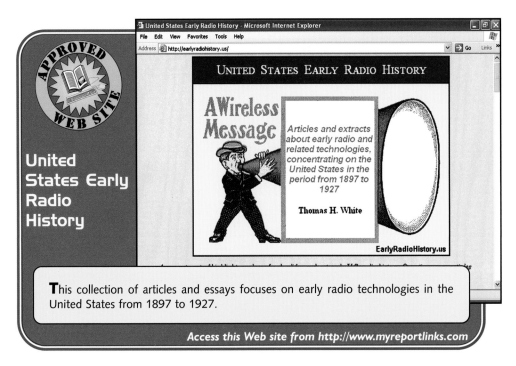

United States Early Radio History

UNITED STATES EARLY RADIO HISTORY

A Wireless Message

Articles and extracts about early radio and related technologies, concentrating on the United States in the period from 1897 to 1927

Thomas H. White

EarlyRadioHistory.us

This collection of articles and essays focuses on early radio technologies in the United States from 1897 to 1927.

Access this Web site from http://www.myreportlinks.com

⊕ SAVING LIVES AND CATCHING CRIMINALS

Wireless was clearly becoming useful. In 1909, a ship called the *Republic* crashed in the Atlantic with another ship. The *Republic's* wireless equipment was damaged, but the operator was not injured. He worked quickly to repair the Marconi equipment and radioed the shore. Ships were sent to rescue the passengers. Approximately seventeen hundred of them were saved as the *Republic* sank into the ocean waters. Wireless equipment had accomplished exactly what Marconi envisioned it would do: save lives.

Marconi's equipment was also used to catch criminals. In 1910, the captain of a ship called the *Montrose* noticed that one of his passengers resembled a photo he had seen in a newspaper weeks earlier. The photo had shown a murder suspect named Hawley Harvey Crippen. The captain, Henry Kendall, knew his passenger was Crippen.

Kendall sent a wireless message to Canada, where the ship was headed. Crippen, who was using a fake name, had no idea that Kendall knew who he actually was. And he certainly did not suspect that the captain had radioed ahead about him. In fact, during the trip, Crippen had remarked to Kendall, "What a wonderful invention wireless is!"[1] But that invention got him

Read about how Marconi's wireless equipment helped to catch Hawley Harvey Crippen, a murder suspect, in 1910. Access a biography of Marconi, an interactive timeline, photos, sound and film clips, newspaper articles, and more on **Marconi Calling**.

EDITOR'S CHOICE

caught. When the ship docked, Crippen was quickly arrested.

➲ TALE OF THE *TITANIC*

One event in which the Marconi equipment played a key role is still famous today. On April 10, 1912, the *Titanic* set sail from England to New York. The ship was brand new, the fanciest in the world, and was said to be unsinkable. The *Titanic's* two Marconi operators, Jack Phillips and Harold Bride, worked throughout the day and night sending messages from the ship's wealthy passengers to shore.

Late on the night of April 14, Phillips received a message from another Marconi operator, Cyrus Evans. Evans was aboard the *Californian,* only ten miles away. He warned Phillips that there was ice in the water. Phillips, thinking the *Titanic* was unsinkable, wasn't too alarmed. He shared the ice warning with the captain, but he asked Evans not to get in touch anymore. Phillips had too much work to do and didn't want to be distracted. Evans got the message, switched his radio off, and went to bed.

Around midnight, Phillips and Bride received word that the *Titanic* had scraped against an iceberg. The jagged ice punched several holes through the side of the ship. The captain ordered the Marconi operators to send out a "CQD"—code for a distress call. The *Titanic* needed help, and fast. The mammoth ship was sinking!

The nearest ship to hear the distress call was the *Carpathia*, which was 58 miles away. "What's wrong?" wrote back the *Carpathia's* wireless operator, Harold Cottam. "Should I tell my captain?"

"Yes," answered Jack. "It's a CQD, old man. We have hit a berg and we are sinking."[2]

As the *Titanic's* crew lowered as many passengers as possible into lifeboats, water poured into the ship. Shortly after two in the morning, the *Titanic* split in half and sank into the Atlantic. Fifteen hundred people died. Another seven hundred floated in lifeboats nearby. Within hours, the *Carpathia* arrived

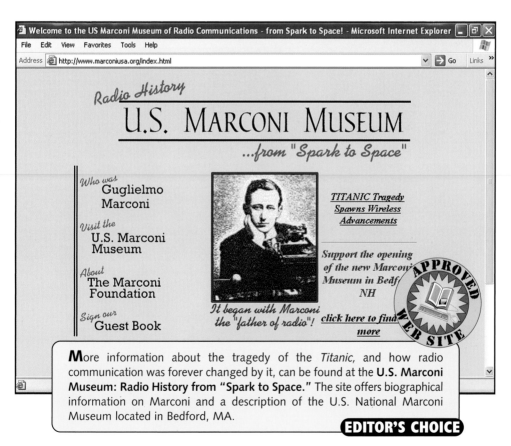

Welcome to the US Marconi Museum of Radio Communications - from Spark to Space! - Microsoft Internet Explorer

File Edit View Favorites Tools Help

Address http://www.marconiusa.org/index.html

Radio History

U.S. MARCONI MUSEUM
...from "Spark to Space"

Who was
Guglielmo
Marconi

Visit the
U.S. Marconi
Museum

About
The Marconi
Foundation

Sign our
Guest Book

It began with Marconi the "father of radio"!

TITANIC Tragedy Spawns Wireless Advancements

Support the opening of the new Marconi Museum in Bedford, NH

click here to find more

APPROVED WEB SITE

More information about the tragedy of the *Titanic*, and how radio communication was forever changed by it, can be found at the **U.S. Marconi Museum: Radio History from "Spark to Space."** The site offers biographical information on Marconi and a description of the U.S. National Marconi Museum located in Bedford, MA.

EDITOR'S CHOICE

An artist's impression of the Titanic *sinking in April 1912 after the ocean liner struck an iceberg in thick fog off Newfoundland. More than 1,500 lives were lost in the tragedy. But 700 people were saved, due in part to the role played by Marconi's wireless technology.*

to save them—thanks to Marconi's technology. Without wireless, no ship would have known to search for the *Titanic,* and it's likely that several hundred more people would have died.

As the *Carpathia* headed for New York, the ship's wireless operator, Harold Cottam, started sending names of survivors to shore. After working around the clock with no sleep, Cottam was too tired to continue. Harold Bride, who had survived the sinking, took over. (Jack Phillips died in the sinking.)

Marconi had been scheduled to travel on the *Titanic,* but luckily his plans changed. When the *Carpathia* reached New York, Marconi was waiting

▽ Harold Bride, the surviving wireless operator of the Titanic, is shown being carried up a ramp of a ship with his feet bandaged in this photo from 1912.

Lee de Forest, Edwin Howard Armstrong, and David Sarnoff are featured as the three legendary figures behind the development of radio on **Empire of the Air**, a PBS companion site to Ken Burns's *American Stories* program. Guglielmo Marconi's contributions are also covered, and the site includes footage from the film and an essay on radio.

for it. He slipped aboard the ship and sought out Bride and Cottam. Marconi wanted to thank them. In the tale of the *Titanic,* history has thanked Marconi, too. His invention saved hundreds of lives, and he was treated like a hero. "Everyone seems too grateful to wireless," he wrote at the time. "I can't go about New York without being mobbed and cheered—worse than Italy."[3]

⟳ WIRELESS GROWS

Following the *Titanic* disaster, the United States created laws requiring all ships at sea to have

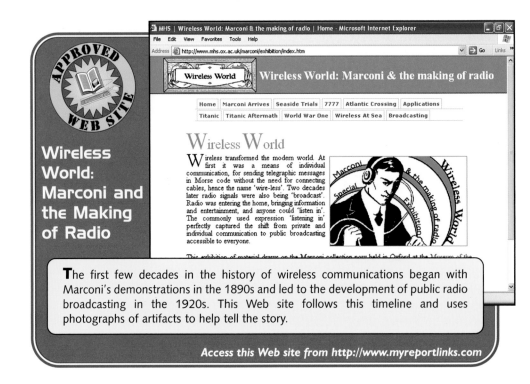

MHS | Wireless World: Marconi & the making of radio | Home - Microsoft Internet Explorer

File Edit View Favorites Tools Help

Address http://www.mhs.ox.ac.uk/marconi/exhibition/index.htm

Wireless World

Wireless World: Marconi & the making of radio

Home | Marconi Arrives | Seaside Trials | 7777 | Atlantic Crossing | Applications
Titanic | Titanic Aftermath | World War One | Wireless At Sea | Broadcasting

Wireless World

Wireless transformed the modern world. At first it was a means of individual communication, for sending telegraphic messages in Morse code without the need for connecting cables, hence the name 'wire-less'. Two decades later radio signals were also being 'broadcast'. Radio was entering the home, bringing information and entertainment, and anyone could 'listen in'. The commonly used expression 'listening in' perfectly captured the shift from private and individual communication to public broadcasting accessible to everyone.

This exhibition of material drawn on the Marconi collection now held in Oxford at the Museum of the

Wireless World: Marconi and the Making of Radio

The first few decades in the history of wireless communications began with Marconi's demonstrations in the 1890s and led to the development of public radio broadcasting in the 1920s. This Web site follows this timeline and uses photographs of artifacts to help tell the story.

Access this Web site from http://www.myreportlinks.com

operators on radio watch twenty-four hours a day. While passenger and shipping vessels used wireless for safety reasons, the militaries found use for the technology as well. Wireless allowed the captains and pilots to communicate in both peace and battle. Military leaders could plan attacks more carefully. Pilots and captains could warn peers about possible dangers. When a plane or ship was damaged, a call for help could be sent. For all these reasons, Marconi's wireless equipment became a key component of military machinery.

Meanwhile, other wireless experts were developing the technology into what we now call radio. That started during the same time period as when

Marconi was marketing wireless equipment to governments and the military. On Christmas Eve 1906, for example, wireless operators turned on their equipment and listened to the holiday song "O Holy Night." It was being broadcast by Canadian businessman Reginald Fessenden, who saw great potential in transmitting entertainment over the airwaves. Fessenden, like Tesla, had worked for Thomas Edison early in his career.

The businessman most responsible for turning radio into a popular household product was David Sarnoff. First an operator of wireless equipment, Sarnoff had been on duty atop the Woolworth Building in New York when the *Titanic* sank. He picked up the ship's distress calls and relayed them to the world. Later, Sarnoff grew close to Marconi and became an officer within his company.

Sarnoff envisioned small electronic boxes that people could buy at the store, gather around at home, and use to listen to news and music. By the 1920s, his vision became real. Marconi's company had become the Radio Corporation of America (RCA), and Sarnoff was running it. RCA manufactured radios and broadcast the programs for customers to hear. Radio was the craze of America. Nearly a century later, along with television and the Internet, it remains a vital part of people's lives.

PERSONAL CHALLENGES

Before he even turned thirty, Marconi was famous and rich. He spent plenty of time in the company of world leaders, including the heads of Russia, Italy, and Germany, and famous inventors like Alexander Graham Bell and Thomas Edison.

Marconi had stylish and famous friends, but wireless was number one in his life. Twice he had been engaged and broken it off. He did not even attend the funeral of his father, who died in 1904. Still, Marconi wanted more out of life. He once said, "A man cannot live on glory alone."[1]

After a handful of romances, Marconi was married on March 16, 1905, to a nineteen-year-old Irish woman named Beatrice O'Brien. Their marriage wasn't a happy one. Beatrice did not like traveling to cold places like Nova Scotia, where Marconi had a wireless station. He did not

CHAPTER 20

spend a lot of time with her, either, and often was interested in other women. Tragically, their first child, Lucia, died a few weeks after she was born in February 1906. The Marconis had three more children: daughters Degna (1908) and Gioia (1916), and son Giulio (1910). Their marriage lasted for eighteen years, but it was rarely—if ever—a happy one.

Throughout his life, Marconi poured his deepest passion into his work. He continued to take risks and make diffi-cult decisions. When his company had financial troubles in 1908, he fired one hundred and fifty workers to save costs. Marconi put his per-sonal money into the company and restored it to financial health.

In 1909, Marconi was awarded the Nobel Prize for his work in radio. Though he was hon-ored to win the award, Marconi was frustrated that the panel made him share it with one of

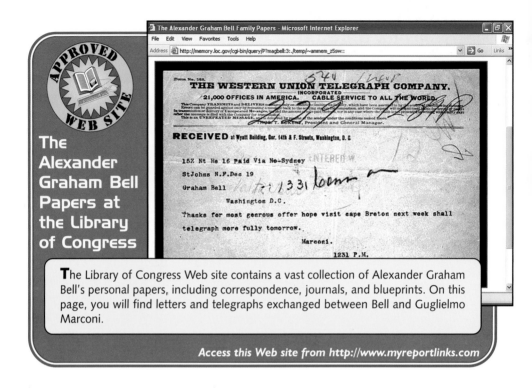

The
Alexander
Graham Bell
Papers at
the Library
of Congress

The Library of Congress Web site contains a vast collection of Alexander Graham Bell's personal papers, including correspondence, journals, and blueprints. On this page, you will find letters and telegraphs exchanged between Bell and Guglielmo Marconi.

Access this Web site from http://www.myreportlinks.com

his chief radio rivals, Karl Ferdinand Braun of Germany.

Marconi had many competitors. Perhaps the toughest was the inventor Sir Oliver Lodge, who had an excellent chance of proving in court that Marconi's company needed to pay him royalties for the right to produce transmitters. Rather than fighting Lodge in court, the Marconi company bought his patent in 1910.

➥ CHALLENGING TIMES

The decade following the *Titanic's* sinking was a difficult one for Marconi. During the summer of 1912, an automobile accident damaged his right

Marconi and his first wife, Beatrice, are shown in a shipboard photo taken in approximately 1920.

History of Communications - RADIO: The Power that Made Radio Realistic - Microsoft Internet Explorer

File   Edit   View   Favorites   Tools   Help

Address http://www.fcc.gov/omd/history/radio/power.html   Go   Links

FCC Federal
Communications
Commission

FCC Home | Search | Updates | E-Filing | Initiatives | For Consumers | Find People

Communications History

FCC > OMD > History > Radio > Power   site map

**FCC: Radio
Pioneers
and Core
Technologies**

Search:
____ Go
Help | Advanced

History Home

The Internet: A Short
History of Getting
Connected

Radio Pioneers &
Core Technologies

  The Ideas that Made
  Radio Possible

  **The Power that Made
  Radio Realistic**

  The Quality that Made
  Radio Popular

The Power that Made Radio Realistic

In 1909, when Marconi shared the Nobel Prize for Physics with Karl Braun, there was no question about the many significant innovations he had brought to the world of wireless radio. There was also no question that his achievements would likely not have been so great if not for the pioneering energy generation work done by Nikola Tesla, whom some consider the real father of radio.

Tesla, a Serbian-American of wide-ranging interests, immigrated to the United States at the age of 28 having already thought through one of his greatest scientific contributions - how to best use alternating current. Since Thomas Edison's company (later General Electric) was the primary advocate for and builder of direct current systems in the United States, it was natural that upon his arrival Tesla first went to work for Edison. But it was not long before the ...nating-

The site is split into three essays: the ideas that made radio possible, the power that made radio realistic, and the quality that made radio popular. Interesting photographs and good links make this site a comprehensive resource.

Access this Web site from http://www.myreportlinks.com

eye so badly that doctors had to remove it. Marconi replaced it with a glass eye. Around the same time, his company had legal troubles. One of Marconi's top assistants was accused of making a deal with the British government and then sharing the information with people who could profit from it. Sharing such inside information is illegal. Though his company was ultimately cleared and suffered no punishment, the ordeal was stressful for Marconi.

In 1914, Marconi's company partnered with its chief rival, Telefunken of Germany. But that positive development was followed by more bad news: World War I was beginning. Germany, Austria, and countries under their influence were fighting France, Britain, and their allies, which eventually included Italy and the United States.

The British government took control of Marconi's wireless system. That communication technology could be vital for troops in war. Though many of Germany's wireless stations were wrecked, the Germans still had a powerful station that they used to broadcast information across the world.

Marconi became a lieutenant in the Italian Army. He solved a problem that was hounding fighter pilots, who could not fly a plane and tap out Morse code at the same time. Marconi developed

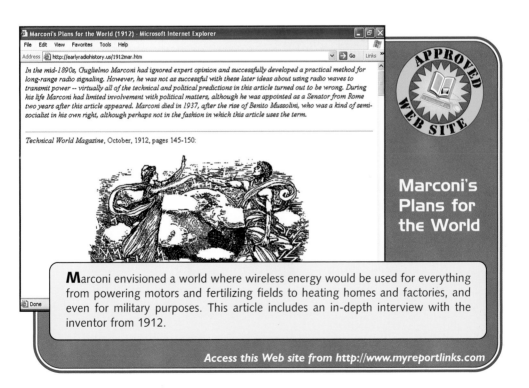

Marconi's Plans for the World (1912) - Microsoft Internet Explorer

File Edit View Favorites Tools Help

Address http://earlyradiohistory.us/1912mar.htm

In the mid-1890s, Guglielmo Marconi had ignored expert opinion and successfully developed a practical method for long-range radio signaling. However, he was not as successful with these later ideas about using radio waves to transmit power -- virtually all of the technical and political predictions in this article turned out to be wrong. During his life Marconi had limited involvement with political matters, although he was appointed as a Senator from Rome two years after this article appeared. Marconi died in 1937, after the rise of Benito Mussolini, who was a kind of semi-socialist in his own right, although perhaps not in the fashion in which this article uses the term.

Technical World Magazine, October, 1912, pages 145-150:

APPROVED WEB SITE

Marconi's Plans for the World

Marconi envisioned a world where wireless energy would be used for everything from powering motors and fertilizing fields to heating homes and factories, and even for military purposes. This article includes an in-depth interview with the inventor from 1912.

Access this Web site from http://www.myreportlinks.com

This photo from 1925 shows the long wave transmitter masts at a Marconi radio station in Berne, Switzerland.

wireless equipment that broadcast voices. Now, the pilots could speak to their ground command. Militaries today still use this voice communication, though the technology has improved considerably. (In Marconi's day, the pilots' voices only transmitted up to twenty miles.) During the war, Marconi also developed systems for sending coded messages and for detecting enemy radio signals.

→ FLOATING AROUND THE WORLD

After the end of World War I, Marconi bought a yacht. He named it *Elettra* (which means "electricity"), built a laboratory inside, and spent much of his time sailing the world. He conducted experiments in which he transmitted electromagnetic waves underwater. Marconi discovered that the waves bounced back when they hit metal. He figured

BBC News: Profile: Marconi, the Wireless Pioneer

BBC News | SCI/TECH | Profile: Marconi, the wireless pioneer - Microsoft Internet Explorer

File   Edit   View   Favorites   Tools   Help

Address   http://news.bbc.co.uk/1/hi/sci/tech/1702037.stm   Go   Links

BBC NEWS

You are in: Sci/Tech

Front Page Tuesday, 11 December, 2001, 12:44 GMT
World
UK   **Profile: Marconi, the wireless**
UK Politics **pioneer**
Business
Sci/Tech
Health
Education
Entertainment
Talking Point
In Depth
AudioVideo

BBC SPORT
BBC Weather

SERVICES   Marconi (left) making shortwave broadcasts from Rome in 1934
Daily E-mail
News Ticker
Mobiles/PDAs

WATCH/LISTEN
ON THIS STORY
The BBC's Matt Pengelly in Cornwall "Marconi was a mysterious man"

BBC Cornwall
WHERE I LIVE

MARCONI
MILESTONE
100th anniversary

▸ Centenary marked
▸ Cornwall celebrates
▸ Radio passion
▸ Wireless facts

TALKING POINT
▸ What will the next 100

By BBC News Online's Helen Briggs

One hundred years after Marconi's historic transmission, the BBC takes an in-depth look at his life. A podcast of Sir Ambrose Fleming talking about the early days of wireless is also available.

Access this Web site from http://www.myreportlinks.com

this could be useful for captains—it would allow them to detect objects under the water and recognize when other ships were nearby. This technology became known as radar. It has long been an essential tool for ships both in peace and war.

In 1928, Marconi's company merged with cable companies. That ended Marconi's role in his company, which was renamed Cable & Wireless. But the deal also paid Marconi enough money to live on for a long time.

After divorcing Bea five years earlier, Marconi remarried in 1927. With his new wife, Maria Cristina Bezzi Scali, he traveled the world, spending time with presidents and emperors. Marconi became particularly close to the Italian leader Benito Mussolini, who led the Fascist party with a tough and often deadly hand. In 1930, Maria gave birth to Marconi's fourth living child. They named her Elettra, after the yacht.

During the last ten years of his life, starting in 1927, Marconi had frequent trouble with his heart. Doctors told him to relax and not to travel so often, but he rarely listened. Marconi kept traveling and working.

One day in the summer of 1937, he was meeting with a friend about some scientific work. Later that day, he was scheduled to meet with Mussolini. But Marconi was running out of energy, and he knew it. He skipped the meeting with Mussolini and instead went to bed. The next day—July 20, 1937—his heart stopped beating. Guglielmo Marconi, age sixty-three, was dead.

One day later, wireless transmitters around the world were shut off. The two-minute tribute of silence honored the man whose vision had set the world abuzz.

An Active Mind

After Wardenclyffe's demise, Tesla lived on little money. He kept working, designing, and testing inventions in his head. Whenever he could afford to do it, he built the inventions in his lab. He spent time working on a variety of inventions,

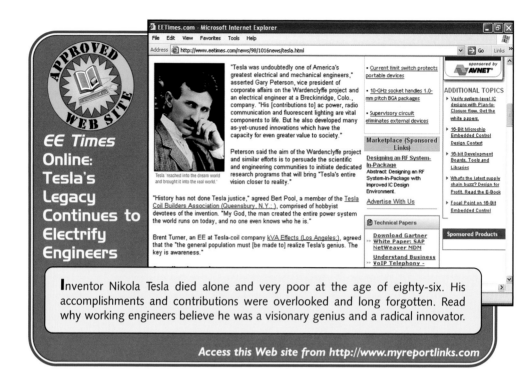

EE Times Online: Tesla's Legacy Continues to Electrify Engineers

Inventor Nikola Tesla died alone and very poor at the age of eighty-six. His accomplishments and contributions were overlooked and long forgotten. Read why working engineers believe he was a visionary genius and a radical innovator.

Access this Web site from http://www.myreportlinks.com

from a small turbine to an airplane motor to an automobile speedometer. He developed ideas for geothermal plants that would run on the earth's heat. He even researched ways to use seaweed to create electricity.

Tesla was remembered. An engineering group gave him the Edison Medal in 1917. He still gave lectures to scientists and interviews to reporters. But success belonged to inventors like Marconi who had been able to match their inventions with strong business decisions.

Tesla lived in a small room in a New York hotel. When he wasn't working, he spent time taking walks. He often fed the pigeons in front of the New York Public Library or even from his window.

Every year on his birthday, Tesla hosted a press conference during which he usually shared with reporters dazzling visions about space and time travel. He made predictions about the future, many of which are already true. Tesla said that people would be able to communicate with pocket-sized equipment. (They do, using cell phones.) He said that people would be able to see news events happen as if they were there. (Television accomplishes that.) He also predicted that the earth's climate would change. (It has, due to global warming.)

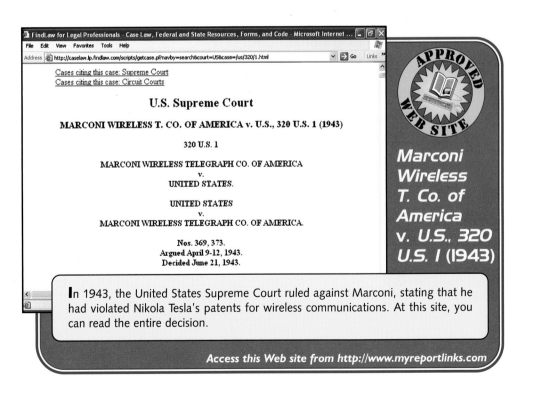

Marconi Wireless T. Co. of America v. U.S., 320 U.S. 1 (1943)

In 1943, the United States Supreme Court ruled against Marconi, stating that he had violated Nikola Tesla's patents for wireless communications. At this site, you can read the entire decision.

Access this Web site from http://www.myreportlinks.com

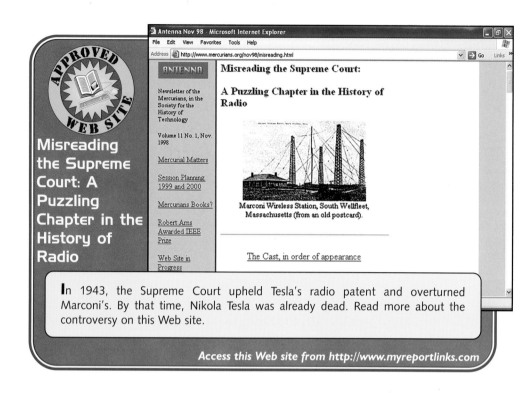

Antenna Nov 98 - Microsoft Internet Explorer

File   Edit   View   Favorites   Tools   Help

Address ☐ http://www.mercurians.org/nov98/misreading.html   ☐ Go   Links »

ANTENNA

Newsletter of the
Mercurians, in the
Society for the
History of
Technology

Volume 11 No. 1, Nov.
1998

Mercurial Matters

Session Planning:
1999 and 2000

Mercurians Books?

Robert Arns
Awarded IEEE
Prize

Web Site in
Progress

Misreading the Supreme Court: A Puzzling Chapter in the History of Radio

Misreading the Supreme Court:

A Puzzling Chapter in the History of Radio

Marconi Wireless Station, South Wellfleet,
Massachusetts (from an old postcard).

The Cast, in order of appearance

In 1943, the Supreme Court upheld Tesla's radio patent and overturned Marconi's. By that time, Nikola Tesla was already dead. Read more about the controversy on this Web site.

Access this Web site from http://www.myreportlinks.com

Tesla died on January 7, 1943, at age eighty-six. People had an appreciation for Tesla's genius while he was alive, but the real honors did not come until years after his death. Beginning with the one hundredth anniversary of his birthday in 1956, schools and awards were named after Tesla. The states of Pennsylvania and Colorado dedicated days and months to him. Tesla was featured on a U.S. postal stamp in 1983. A museum chronicling his life opened in Belgrade. Other museums around the world hosted exhibits on Tesla.

The biggest news, however, came just months after Tesla's death. After many years of challenges and arguments, the U.S. Supreme Court delivered an important decision. It was one that Tesla would have loved. The court decided that Tesla, along with two other inventors, had priority over Marconi in the invention of radio.

In other words, the highest court in the country affirmed what Tesla had long claimed: he was indeed the father (or at least *one* of the fathers) of wireless.

THE LEGACY OF TWO MEN

Nikola Tesla and other inventors made key contributions to wireless, but Guglielmo Marconi's name is the one most often associated with radio. This is largely because of the publicity Marconi received. He was world famous. Crowds cheered him then the way a rock star would be greeted today. His public demonstrations of wireless wowed people and tickled their imaginations. Marconi was driven by fame. He enjoyed it when, as he wrote in letters, people made 'lots more fuss over me than over anyone else."[1]

Tesla was a showman, too. He staged great spectacles and gave entertaining, sometimes

CHAPTER 7

outlandish interviews. He peppered his remarks with end-of-the-world talk. He once claimed his oscillator could chop the earth "as a boy would split an apple—and forever end the career of man."[2] He claimed to have successfully tested his own wireless equipment at a distance of thirty miles in 1896 or 1897, but kept it secret.

Unlike Marconi, Tesla was not a natural businessman. For example, when Marconi used wireless to provide up-to-date results of boat races, he knew the publicity would be good for business. Given the chance to do the same thing, however, Tesla turned it down. He preferred to make his first public demonstration of wireless a massive, worldwide affair. That chance never came. Instead, Marconi staged simpler demonstrations that created newspaper

On this companion site to the PBS series *Tesla: Master of Lightning,* find out why Tesla is considered one of the greatest electrical inventors who ever lived. Discover more about his life and legacy and access an interactive lab, photographs and animations.

EDITOR'S CHOICE

headlines and got people talking. That is one of the primary reasons why he was given so much credit for the invention of radio.[3]

⊖ Stressed Relationship

Marconi and Tesla knew each other, but not well. They met only a few times, and Tesla found Marconi to be frustrating. The friction between them started when William Preece decided to develop a wireless telegraphy system for Britain's post office. He and Tesla had been in contact. Tesla had offered to develop a test model—and that's when Marconi showed up. According to Tesla, Marconi told Preece "that he had tried out [Tesla's] apparatus and that it did not work."[4]

Tesla, not surprisingly, found this troubling. Of course his wireless system could work! He just needed the chance to develop and demonstrate it for a willing audience like Preece. But when Marconi successfully captured Preece's attention with his own wireless system, Tesla's chance was shot.

"Evidently [Marconi] succeeded in his purpose," Tesla said, "for nothing was done in regard to my proposal."[5]

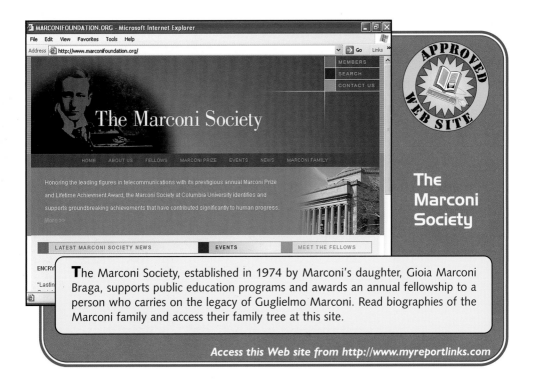

The Marconi Society

The Marconi Society, established in 1974 by Marconi's daughter, Gioia Marconi Braga, supports public education programs and awards an annual fellowship to a person who carries on the legacy of Guglielmo Marconi. Read biographies of the Marconi family and access their family tree at this site.

Access this Web site from http://www.myreportlinks.com

⮕ "Time Will Tell"

Out for dinner one evening in 1900, Marconi and a pair of men stopped by Tesla's New York lab to ask for an explanation of transmitting power over long distances. Marconi listened, then said that Tesla's ideas were impossible.

"Time will tell, Mr. Marconi," Tesla retorted. Marconi and his companions headed for the door.[6]

Despite stressful moments like that, Tesla remained publicly polite when talking about his rival Marconi. "He is a splendid worker, full of rare and subtle energies," Tesla wrote in a letter that was read at a dinner honoring Marconi after the successful transatlantic signal.[7]

But Tesla was inwardly frustrated. Marconi had told Preece that Tesla's equipment did not work, yet here he was *using* it. Marconi had admitted as much. In an article for a publication

This monument to Nikola Tesla at the observation deck to Niagara Falls, New York, is the work of Croatian sculptor Frane Krsinic. It was given by Yugoslavia to the United States in 1976, as a gift in celebration of Tesla's design of the first hydroelectric power plant in Niagara Falls.

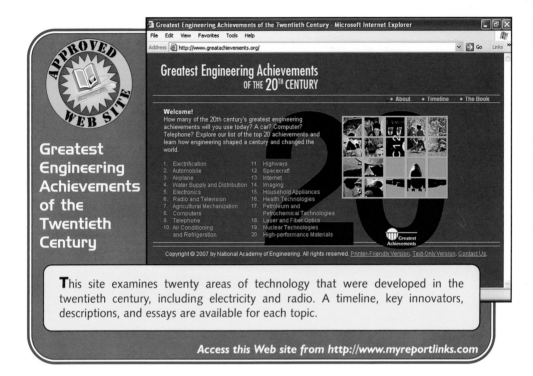

Greatest
Engineering
Achievements
of the
Twentieth
Century

Greatest Engineering Achievements of the Twentieth Century - Microsoft Internet Explorer

File Edit View Favorites Tools Help

Address http://www.greatachievements.org/   Go   Links »

Greatest Engineering Achievements
OF THE 20TH CENTURY

◆ About   ◆ Timeline   ◆ The Book

Welcome!
How many of the 20th century's greatest engineering achievements will you use today? A car? Computer? Telephone? Explore our list of the top 20 achievements and learn how engineering shaped a century and changed the world.

1. Electrification
2. Automobile
3. Airplane
4. Water Supply and Distribution
5. Electronics
6. Radio and Television
7. Agricultural Mechanization
8. Computers
9. Telephone
10. Air Conditioning and Refrigeration
11. Highways
12. Spacecraft
13. Internet
14. Imaging
15. Household Appliances
16. Health Technologies
17. Petroleum and Petrochemical Technologies
18. Laser and Fiber Optics
19. Nuclear Technologies
20. High-performance Materials

Greatest Achievements

This site examines twenty areas of technology that were developed in the twentieth century, including electricity and radio. A timeline, key innovators, descriptions, and essays are available for each topic.

Access this Web site from http://www.myreportlinks.com

called the *Electrical Review,* Marconi wrote about using a Tesla coil to produce oscillations, or vibrations in the air. Tesla, who was riding a train when he read the article, was so shocked that he spilled his coffee. Was this the same Marconi who said Tesla's equipment did not work?

Tesla realized then that he was in a race with Marconi for wireless domination of the world. "I could not develop the business slowly," he later wrote. Let Marconi report on yacht races, he figured. Tesla focused on Wardenclyffe, his world communications center. But when Marconi sent his signal across the Atlantic, it meant the end of Tesla's chance to take the wireless market.[8]

Tesla spent the rest of his life knowing that Marconi had captured glory in which he should have shared. He still avoided criticizing Marconi, though in 1927, he said, "Mr. Marconi is a donkey."[9]

Tesla and Marconi were different men driven by the same goal. They both wanted wireless to reach around the world. At that, they succeeded.

RADIO EXPERIMENTS
ACTIVITY #1

 **MAKING WAVES[1]**

Radio waves surround us all the time. You can create them, too, by using a few simple tools.

MATERIALS:

- **AM radio**
- **new 9-volt battery**
- **a coin**

Step 1: Turn on your AM radio. (If yours is an AM/FM radio, be sure to flip on the AM dial.) Tune it to a place where you hear nothing but static. You will find this in the areas on the dial that separate your local stations.

Step 2: Hold the battery a few inches from the radio's antenna.

Step 3: Use your coin to quickly click the terminals on your battery. Do this fast—just a tap. Listen to your radio carefully: You should hear a short "click" in the static. This happens because you are briefly turning your battery "on" by connecting the two terminals.

QUESTIONS:

- **Try different coins to see if some types of metal work better than others.**

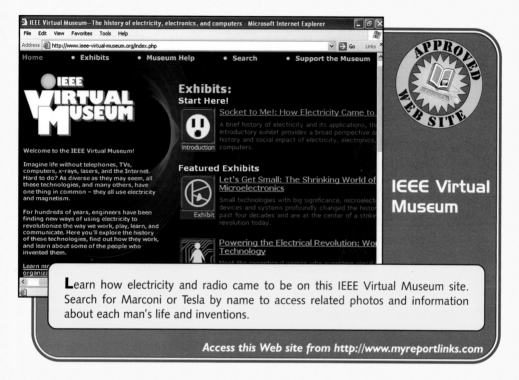

Learn how electricity and radio came to be on this IEEE Virtual Museum site. Search for Marconi or Tesla by name to access related photos and information about each man's life and inventions.

Access this Web site from http://www.myreportlinks.com

- **You can tap coded messages using this technique. Try sending a message in Morse code, or create your own coded language.**

MAKE AN ELECTROMAGNET[2]

Electricity creates a magnetic field. Electromagnets are a key component of most electrical products, including radios. While he was experimenting with wireless transmission in the attic of his childhood home, Guglielmo Marconi used an electromagnet. He also used a coherer—a glass tube with metal filings—to conduct electricity.

⊜MATERIALS:

- **an iron nail, three inches or longer**
- **three feet or more of copper wire, with thin insulation**
- **masking or duct tape**
- **D battery**
- **paper clips or iron filings**
- **a thin test tube**

Step 1: Wrap your copper wire around the nail in neat, tight spirals. The wraps should touch one another like coils on a compressed spring, but they should not overlap. Leave eight to ten inches of wire hanging off each side of the nail.

Step 2: If you have a lot of extra wire hanging off the nail, cut it so that both sides have eight to ten inches. Remove about an inch of insulation from each end.

Step 3: Use the tape to connect one end of the wire to the positive end of the battery and the other end of the wire to the battery's negative pole.

Step 4: When both ends of the wire are connected to the battery, you have an electromagnet. Use the nail to attract paper clips.

Step 5: Put some iron filings in the test tube and cap the end. Make sure the filings are loose— don't pack them too tight.

Step 6: Try to make the iron filings cohere (or stick together) by using your electromagnet.

Points of caution: Be safe and be clean! When connected, your battery may become hot. Make sure your electromagnet is far away from wall outlets and other open sources of electricity. And be cautious with iron filings—they are very messy.

→ QUESTIONS:

The electricity flowing from the battery through the wires aligns all the molecules in your nail in the same direction. When this happens, the nail becomes magnetized.

- **How much can you pick up? The stronger your electromagnet, the more paper clips your nail will attract. Likewise, the iron filings should clump more tightly.**

- **To strengthen your electromagnet, wrap a second layer of wire on top of the original coils. Be careful again to wrap the wires tightly and in the same direction, not overlapping.**

- **Disconnect one end of the wire. The paper clips should fall off or the iron filings should stop cohering. Your electromagnet works only when the electricity flows through it. Otherwise, it is not a magnet— just a nail wrapped in wire.**

Marconi used this same on-and-off technique with his wireless equipment. When the magnet was turned "on," the wireless emitted radio waves. When the magnet was disconnected, the waves stopped transmitting.

Report Links

The Internet sites described below can be accessed at http://www.myreportlinks.com

▶**Marconi Calling**
Editor's Choice Visit this interactive Web site to learn more about Guglielmo Marconi.

▶*Tesla: Master of Lightning*
Editor's Choice PBS explores the life and accomplishments of Nikola Tesla.

▶**U.S. Marconi Museum: Radio History from "Spark to Space"**
Editor's Choice The Guglielmo Marconi Foundation's Web site about Marconi and the history of radio.

▶**The Case Files: Nikola Tesla**
Editor's Choice Read about Nikola Tesla's inventions on this Web site.

▶**Nikola Tesla Museum**
Editor's Choice Take an online tour of this fascinating museum devoted to Tesla.

▶**BBC: Marconi 100**
Editor's Choice This BBC Web site celebrates a century of radio.

▶**The Alexander Graham Bell Papers at the Library of Congress**
View letters and telegraphs exchanged by Marconi and Bell.

▶**American Heritage: The Cable Under the Sea**
This detailed article tells of the twelve-year struggle to lay the transatlantic cable.

▶**BBC News: Profile: Marconi, the Wireless Pioneer**
This profile of Marconi provides a good overview of his accomplishments.

▶*EE Times* **Online: Tesla's Legacy Continues to Electrify Engineers**
Find out why electrical engineers view Nikola Tesla as a hero in this *EE Times* article.

▶**Empire of the Air**
A close look is given to the story of radio's early days.

▶**FCC: Radio Pioneers and Core Technologies**
The FCC presents information on radio's technological breakthroughs and key inventors on this site.

▶**Greatest Engineering Achievements of the Twentieth Century**
This National Academy of Engineering Web site celebrates inventors and technological achievement.

▶**The Great Transatlantic Cable**
This PBS documentary and companion Web site are about the laying of the transatlantic cable.

▶**Guglielmo Marconi: Radio Star**
Physics World magazine offers this in-depth examination of Marconi's life.

Report Links

The Internet sites described below can be accessed at
http://www.myreportlinks.com

▶**IEEE Virtual Museum**
IEEE's Virtual Museum explores the beginnings of electricity and radio.

▶**Invent Now**
On this site, browse a database of inventors and learn how to patent your own invention.

▶**Marconi**
Memorial University of Newfoundland offers this article on Marconi.

▶**Marconi History**
A comprehensive timeline of Marconi's life is available on this site.

▶**The Marconi Society**
This organization keeps the legacy of Marconi alive.

▶**Marconi's Plans for the World**
A 1912 *Technical World Magazine* article about Marconi and his vision of wireless technology.

▶*Marconi Wireless T. Co. of America v. U.S., 320 U.S. 1* (1943)
The full text of the 1943 Supreme Court decision regarding some of Marconi's patents.

▶**Misreading the Supreme Court: A Puzzling Chapter in the History of Radio**
This article looks at who really invented radio.

▶**Selected Tesla Writings**
Learn more about electricity at this site.

▶**Tesla Memorial Society of New York**
This Web site commemorates Nikola Tesla.

▶**Timeline of Marconi Century**
This timeline covers 1874–2004.

▶**TWP Nikola Tesla Photo Archive**
View this collection of Tesla-related images.

▶**United States Early Radio History**
This Web site offers an introduction to early radio.

▶**Villa Griffone: The Birthplace of Wireless**
Take an online tour of Marconi's home and laboratory.

▶**Wireless World: Marconi and the Making of Radio**
This University of Oxford online exhibition explores the making of radio.

alternating current—Electric current that moves up and down, like a roller coaster, as it travels in one direction.

apparatus—A group of instruments or machinery.

armature—A usually rotating part of an electric machine that consists of coils of wire wrapped around a metal core.

contraption—Another word for a machine or device. Also, apparatus.

direct current—Electric current that travels straight and in one direction.

dynamo—An electric generator.

electromagnetic—When an electric current produces magnetic action.

entrepreneur—One who launches, manages, and assumes the risks of an enterprise or business venture.

frequency—The number of times a radio wave moves up and down when compared to other radio waves. Waves broadcast at different frequencies so they will not interfere with one another.

generator—A machine in which energy that has been created by machines is changed into electrical energy.

ionosphere—The part of the earth's atmosphere that is electrically charged.

patent—A legal document that names the creator of an invention. The owner of a patent is allowed to sell the invention.

receiver—A device that takes the signals sent by a transmitter and changes them into audio or visual form.

royalty—In the sciences, a payment that goes to the inventor each time a copy of his or her patented device is sold.

telegraph—An electronic system for sending messages.

transatlantic—Something that crosses the Atlantic Ocean.

transmitter—An apparatus that sends signals by air waves or over a wire.

turbine—A machine with a rotor that is spun by water.

voltage—The measurement of electrical power when expressed in volts. A device with a high voltage means that it has a lot of volts, or units of electrical power.

Chapter 1. A Transatlantic Plan

1. Stephen Hall, "Tesla: a scientific saint, wizard, or carnival sideman?" *Smithsonian,* June 1986, p. 128.

Chapter 2. Smart Young Scientists

1. Donald G. Schueler, "Inventor Marconi: brilliant, dapper, tough to live with," *Smithsonian,* March 1982, p. 134.

2. Nikola Tesla and Ben Johnston (intro.), *My Inventions: The Autobiography of Nikola Tesla* (Williston, Vt.: Hart Brothers, 1982), p. 54.

Chapter 3. Wireless Works!

1. Erik Larson, *Thunderstruck* (New York: Crown Publishing, 2006) Accessed online at: <http://www.randomhouse.com/crown/thunderstruck /excerpt.html> (May 29, 2007).

2. *"Meeting with Preece,"* Archive section 4, n.d., <http://www.marconicalling.com/introsting .htm> (June 16, 2007).

3. R. W. Simons, "Guglielmo Marconi and Early Systems of Wireless Communication," *GEC Review,* Vol. 11, No. 1, 1996, <http:// www.radarpages.co.uk/ download/p37.pdf>, see p. 45 of PDF (June 20, 2007).

4. Gavin Weightman, *Signor Marconi's Magic Box* (Cambridge, Mass.: Perseus Books Group/Da Capo Press, 2003), (Reprinted by HarperCollins Publishers.), p. 60.

5. Ibid., p. 74.

6. Ibid., p. 100.

Chapter 4. Powerful Visions

1. Nikola Tesla and Ben Johnston (intro.), *My Inventions: The Autobiography of Nikola Tesla* (Williston, Vt.: Hart Brothers, 1982), p. 57.

2. Ibid., p. 65.

3. *"Life and Legacy," "Coming to America"* section, n.d., <http://www.pbs.org/tesla/index.html> (April 3, 2007).

4. Stephen Hall, "Tesla: a scientific saint, wizard, or carnival sideman?" *Smithsonian,* June 1986, p. 125.

5. Margaret Cheney, *Tesla: Man Out of Time* (New York: Simon & Schuster, 2001) as quoted on <http://www.lucidcafe.com/library/currentread/currentread04/html> (May 21, 2007).

6. Eliot Marshall, "Seeking Redress for Nikola Tesla," *Science,* October 30, 1981, pp. 523–525.

7. Ibid., p. 524.

8. Gavin Weightman, *Signor Marconi's Magic Box* (Cambridge, Mass.: Perseus Books Group/ Da Capo Press, 2003), (Reprinted by HarperCollins Publishers), p. 109.

Chapter 5. Wireless Becomes Widespread

1. *"Dr. Crippen: The Chase,"* Archive section 4, n.d., <http://www.marconicalling.com/introsting.htm> (April 23, 2007).

2. Gavin Weightman, *Signor Marconi's Magic Box* (Cambridge, Mass.: Perseus Books Group/ Da Capo Press, 2003), (Reprinted by HarperCollins Publishers), p. 249.

3. Ibid., p. 254.

Chapter 6. Personal Challenges

1. Media Matrix, "Guglielmo Marconi: A Voice From Beyond the Void," 2006, <http://www.worldofbiography.com/9063-Guglielmo%20Marconi/life3.htm> (May 3, 2007).

Chapter 7. The Legacy of Two Men

1. Donald G. Schueler, "Inventor Marconi: brilliant, dapper, tough to live with." *Smithsonian,* March 1982, p. 137.

2. Stephen Hall, "Tesla: a scientific saint, wizard, or carnival sideman?" *Smithsonian,* June 1986, p. 122.

3. Marc J. Seifer, *Wizard: The Life and Times of Nikola Tesla* (New York: Kensington Publishing Group, 1998), p. 187.

4. Ibid., pp. 172–173.

5. Ibid., p. 173.

6. Ibid., p. 237.

7. Ibid., p. 278.

8. Ibid., pp. 262–263.

9. Ibid., p. 130.

Radio Experiments

1. Marshall Brain, "How Radio Works," n.d., <http://www.howstuffworks.com> (May 20, 2007)

2. Experiment drawn from others posted at <http://www.sciencebob.com> and <http://www.kidscanmakeit.com>.

Aldrich, Lisa J. *Nikola Tesla and the Taming of Electricity.* Greenboro, N.C.: Morgan Reynolds Publishers, 2005.

Bankston, John. *Alexander Graham Bell and the Story of the Telephone.* Hockessin, Del.: Mitchell Lane Publishers, 2005.

Burgan, Michael. *Thomas Alva Edison: Great American Inventor.* Minneapolis: Compass Point Books, 2006.

Carlson, Laurie. *Thomas Edison for Kids: His Life and Ideas: Twenty-one Activities.* Chicago: Chicago Review Press, 2006.

Hegedus, Alannah, and Kaitlin Rainey. *Bleeps and Blips to Rocket Ships: Great Inventions in Communications.* Toronto: Tundra Books, 2001.

Parker, Steve. *1900–1920: A Shrinking World.* Milwaukee, Wis.: Gareth Stevens Pub., 2001.

Platt, Richard. *Eureka! Great Inventions and How They Happened.* Boston: Kingfisher, 2003.

Shell, Barry. *Sensational Scientists: The Journeys and Discoveries of 24 Men and Women of Science.* Vancouver: Raincoast Books, 2005.

Sherrow, Victoria. *Guglielmo Marconi: Inventor of Radio and Wireless Communication.* Berkeley Heights, N.J.: Enslow Publishers, 2004.

Sonneborn, Liz. *Guglielmo Marconi: Inventor of Wireless Technology.* New York: Franklin Watts, 2005.

Index

A
AC. *See* alternating current (AC).
Adams, Edward Dean, 68
alternating current (AC)
  breakthrough, 51
  criticism of, 59
  funding issues, 57
  motor, 52, 58
  patents, 58–60
  research, 6, 49–51
  usefulness of, 67
  World's Fair
    demonstration, 66
arc lighting, 57

B
Batchelor, Charles, 52, 56
Bell, Alexander Graham, 47, 92
Braun, Karl Ferdinand, 94
Bride, Harold, 84, 88
Brown, A. K., 57–58
Buffalo, New York, 67–69

C
Cable & Wireless, 100
Campbell-Swinton, A. A., 38
cell phones, 103
climate change, 103
communication
  pre-radio, 10–11, 28
  wireless (*See* wireless
    communications)
communications city, 74–77
Continental Edison Company, 51–52
Cottam, Harold, 85, 88
criminals, catching, 82–84
Crippen, Hawley Harvey, 82–84

D
direct current (DC), 49, 56, 59, 67
ditches, digging, 57

E
Edison, Thomas, 6, 52–57, 64, 91

Edison Medal honors, 7, 49, 102
the Egg of Columbus, *65*
electricity
  activities, 115–117
  in earth's atmosphere, 33, 36, 64
  equipment patents, Tesla, 58, *59*
  study of, by Marconi, 21, 29, 33–36, 38
  study of, by Tesla, 27, 49–51, 61–64, 71–74, 102
electromagnetic wave
  experiments, 6, 29, 31–36, 99–100
electromagnets, 115–117
Evans, Cyrus, 84

F
Farraday, Michael, 29
Fessenden, Reginald, 91
France, 7, 44

G
global warming, 103
Great Britain, 6, 7, 44

H
Hertz, Heinrich, 6, 29
Higher Real Gymnasium, 6, 26–27

I
induction motor, *58*
insider trading, 96
ionosphere, 36, 64
Isle of Wight, 42–43

J
Jameson-Davis, Henry, 38, 41

K
Kemp, George, 44, 47
Kendall, Henry, 82–84

L
Leghorn Technical Institute, 6, 21
lighting systems, issues with, 53–56

126